1979

ENIGMA

Also by the author:

Dream Reality:
The Conscious Creation of Dream
and Paranormal Experience

Singularities
Advances in psychology, parapsychology,
medicine & the humanities
(a newsletter)

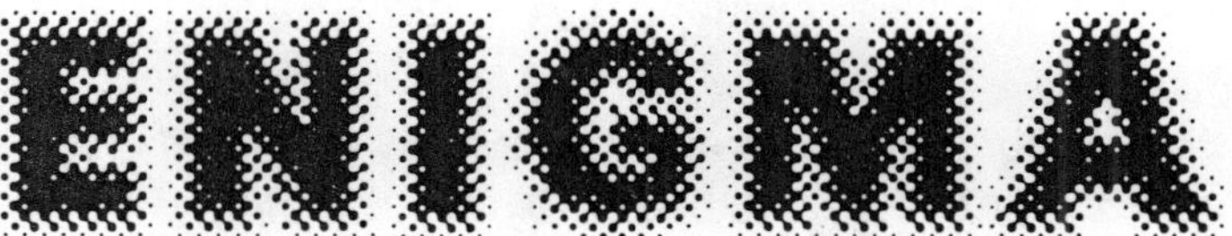

ENIGMA

Psychology, the Paranormal and Self-Transformation

James J. Donahoe

BENCH PRESS
P.O. Box 24635
Oakland, California 94623
U.S.A.

Bench Press
P.O. Box 24635
Oakland, CA 94623
USA

Additional copies available from the publisher.
(Add $1.00 to book price for shipping.)

Paperback Cover:

Design: Anne Morrison
Photograph: Scott Morrison
Airbrushing: Gary Fox

Publisher's recommended subject categories:
1. Consciousness. 2. Dreams. 3. Psychical research.

Library of Congress Cataloging in Publication Data

Donahoe, James J
  Enigma.

  Bibliography: p.
  Includes index.
  1. Psychical research. I. Title.
BF1031.D655   133.8   79-12874
ISBN 0-916534-08-1
ISBN 0-916534-09-X pbk.

Manufactured in the United States of America

for my sister
Joan,
an explorer in her own right
who has among her gifts,
a sense of humor

Acknowledgments

I would like to express my appreciation for the tremendous help Pam Yellen has given me in regard to ENIGMA, not only for the voyages she initiated (some of them described in these pages), but also for the talented and time-devouring effort she placed into the editorial and production aspects of the book.

Heidi Orbach and Stephen Ludwig contributed their energies and time to much of the work needed to complete the final stages of the book's preparation. I appreciate their generous assistance, especially on those projects which arose suddenly and required quick action.

Stephen Arnold inspired me in our many brainstorming sessions. He also advised me to revise and add to the book in places I had prematurely considered complete.

I would like to thank my parents, Claire and Joseph Donahoe, for their continuing encouragement and support—all which helped materialize ENIGMA.

Finally, I am grateful for the efforts of my fellow explorers, including my students, without whom this particular individual dream of a book could not have occurred.

Contents

Introduction

The unified perspective I take towards the varied subjects of ENIGMA comes from my realization that paranormal abilities and altered states of consciousness, ''new'' powers and so-called normal perceptions, all reflect the fundamental role of imagination in the structure of human awareness. The current conception of the faculty of imagination needs broadening if the study of psychological and paranormal acts is to progress on a wide scale. Luckily, the phenomena readily lend themselves to this task, for reasons I make clear in the text. It is difficult, if not impossible, to still believe in the hard and fast separation of ''inner'' and ''outer'' events, for example, after you have had the kinds of experiences described here—dreams which you and your friends spontaneously share, and recall in detail afterwards; extraordinary waking/dream intersections in which the two states blend, placing one dreaming person into another's waking state environment (or the other way around, depending upon your perspective); highly specific and accurate telepathic exchanges; and so on.

It may seem that I am stressing the values of personal experimentation in the study of this field, and I am, but I also believe in the importance of developing the full continuum of abilities available to us, analytic discrimination as well as exploration of events beyond the norm. For this reason I include some of the early history of consciousness research, the models developed then and now to handle experimenters' discoveries, and my own insights and proposals.

The adventures and research represented here have led me inexorably to the understanding that special dream types, paranormal abilities, and the myriad other kinds of events which constitute the frontiers of consciousness research demonstrate the boundary-surpassing capacity of human awareness and action, a capacity which can and will provide as many enigmas as anyone could want.

The diverse topics which make up my work and that of others in the field deserve a unified presentation. If limit-transcending capacities form the foundation of such phenomena, as I believe, then perhaps the best tactic for conveying knowledge on the subject is to be as open-ended and comprehensive as possible. At the least, I hope to share with readers an appreciation for the vast avenues of exploration which directly relate to psychology and parapsychology, including those paths not normally associated with these fields. In any case, in keeping with my subject, I have no desire to ''finalize'' the reader's understanding, but I do want, above all, to encourage and inspire it.

Part I:

Tales

of

Adventure

1

Adventures

Awake and Dreaming

To be "lucid" in a dream, in the special sense of the word, means to know you are dreaming while the dream takes place. There are varying degrees of lucidity. You might question whether or not you are dreaming, for example, without reaching a definite conclusion. This, Celia Green labels a "pre-lucid" dream. You might conclude that you are dreaming, but fail to act on that realization. Once lucidity is prolonged enough, you can use that awareness to consciously direct dream events. What happens next is up to you.

One of the major approaches to lucid dreaming is the psychotherapeutic one. In this context, dream lucidity would be used as a vehicle for resolving emotional conflicts. Those people who concentrate on this direction take the position that the important thing about dreams is their psychodynamic content.

An example of therapeutic dreaming: you are in a nightmare, being pursued by some nameless adversary. You become lucid, and decide to turn around and face your opponent. If you can stay calm enough, you might make friends with whatever has been chasing you, or even absorb it into your own identity. If that tactic doesn't work—that is, if the nightmare doesn't resolve itself or becomes worse, you can always wake yourself up. Not all nightmare situations need to be confronted; some may be ignored.

As you work with developing and refining dream lucidity, you may recognize the influence of your emotions upon the dream environment. In many cases, fear creates the nightmare environment, not the other way around. For example, I have become lucid in a number of unpleasant dreams, some of them nightmares, in which lucidity did nothing to dispel my anxiety. From inside the dream, it seemed to me that my dream surroundings justified my fear. After all, the creature *was* after me, wasn't it? But in fact, once I became peaceful, the dream environment followed suit. The same held true for creatures within that environment. These creatures, once threatening in behavior and frightening in appearance, could change into innocuous or even friendly figures.

This principle, that calmness or agitation in people can strongly affect how they perceive their environment, also applies to altered states in general, including psychedelic and out-of-body experience (OOB).[1] Robert Monroe, talking about the latter, described an out-of-body panic he had as a result of the appearance of some serpentine forms, which seemed to be chasing him. In future OOB excursions, Monroe learned that cats appear in serpent form, to him at least, when *they* are out-of-body. The first ''cats'' he met, were apparently just trying to be

[1]During an out-of-the-body experience (OOB), the subject feels herself moving out of her body to another discrete location, while her senses continue intact. The person traveling out-of-body feels spatially present in the new location and often experiences a sharpness and clarity of sensation uncommon in the waking state. See the remarks in the glossary for more information.

affectionate by following him around. Upon later reflection, Monroe realized that the "serpents" looked in some ways like his pet cats, and he says he became able to identify each cat's out-of-body appearance.[2]

The influence of momentary emotions upon the content of psychedelic experience has been well established, so I don't think that further examples are needed here. In all three circumstances—dreaming, OOB's, and internalized psychedelic journeys—the key consists of knowing that intentional relaxation along with compassion directed toward the feared elements in your environment, can be sufficient to transform them.

There are advantages to working out dream therapies. My only disagreement with the psychotherapeutic approach is with the position that dreams are nothing more than reflections of waking state, psychodynamic content, subsidiary to the waking state and totally dependent upon it. You can just as logically assert that the waking state is dependent upon dream events, and proceed to interpret in reverse fashion. Or, more to the point, you can interpret any event, dream or waking, in psychodynamic fashion. In this regard, divination and interpretation are merely different words for the same process.

The same principle that allows dream interpretation to work, also allows for successful *I Ching* castings. What may differ is not the process, but the context; i.e., the question. A psychodynamic context is one of many options available to the questioner, and if the interpretation rendered seems valid, that validity is a demonstration of synchronicity. A Jungian dream interpretation which provides insight, which seems to work, does not prove that dreams are Jungian, any more than does a successful

---

[2]Monroe, author of *Journeys Out of the Body* (See bibliography), related this story during an appearance at the First Unitarian Church in San Francisco, in March, 1974.

Freudian interpretation. Similarly, a parapsychological interpretation which turns up verifiable information does not prove that all dreams are parapsychological.

When I work with my own dreams, or those of someone else, I try to be as flexible as possible, allowing the dream to bring to mind insights ranging from the psychological state of the dreamer to potential parapsychological material, and beyond. I remind myself and my listeners that no dream is reducible to any amount of interpretations of it, and that the same interpretation process can be applied to any memories, not just those concerning dreams. I encourage people to develop a large vocabulary of interpretations, a flexibility of approach, and a realization of the fact that dream experience tends to accommodate the dreamer's interpretive slant. The usefulness of any particular slant, whether psychotherapeutic, paranormal, or some other, depends upon where you want to go.

From my point of view, dreams have no fixed, essential nature. By logical extension, once you consider the operations of synchronicity I referred to a few paragraphs back, and consider, too, the idea that the waking state is no more a discrete "state" than is dreaming, it becomes evident that so-called waking state consciousness has no fixed nature either. You can look at this situation as an indication of fantastic creativity and mobility if you want, just as you can take that stance towards dreaming.

All dreams are valid events in their own right, not just lucid, high[3] or paranormal ones. People who are unwilling to grant validity to all their dreams can at least concede

---

[3]In a "high dream," the dreamer experiences an expanded, altered state of consciousness analogous to psychedelic experience.

that some dreams, notably the precognitive[4] and mutual[5] varieties, do not depend upon waking sensory impressions. Someone who believes firmly in the absolute primacy of those perceptions we call the waking state will not be talked out of it easily, any more than will someone who believes that all aspects of mental life are epiphenomena of the brain. But an accumulation of personal experience with dreams that go beyond that paradigm may loosen things up a bit.[6]

One of the odd possibilities of lucid dreaming is to be in a dream, interpreting events as they take place. In my own case, such interpretation does not change the dream content. I can remember trying to evade a creature out of the depths in one dream—it approached steadily as I attempted to figure out the psychoanalytic spell which would disperse it. No such luck. Finally I confronted and befriended the creature, and we ended up going our separate ways. Our conversation revealed nothing particularly illuminating about my waking, emotional state, though psychoanalysts, given the chance, would no doubt be able to chalk off a quick half-dozen speculations. For me, the encounter with the creature had no ready analogy with the waking state, and didn't need one. The point of the dream was to get out of the original situation, which I did. Further analysis in this case struck me as suspiciously similar to hunting snarks, and I'd found one too many beasts already.

Dreamers working outside of the psychotherapeutic

[4]A ''precognitive dream'' is one which contains fore-knowledge of the future. See the glossary entries for this and other terms.

[5]In a ''mutual dream,'' two or more people share the same dream environment.

[6]My previous book contains methods for evoking such dream experiences. See James J. Donahoe, *Dream Reality: The Conscious Creation of Dream & Paranormal Experience* (Oakland, CA: Bench Press, rev. ed., 1979).

framework have used lucidity as a means to transform the dream into paranormal experience. I discovered that lucid dreams worked very well for obtaining telepathic information during a course of experiments with mutual dreams. The telepathy came unexpectedly. I had been trying to evoke mutual dreams nearly every night with the help of dream lucidity. Once in the dream and fully lucid, I would immediately seek out someone I knew (the person varied). Then that person and I would babble excitedly to each other about how amazing it was that we were meeting in a dream; this was followed by mutual promises to remember the dream encounter upon awakening.

Unfortunately, although I had such dreams often, my dream companions weren't recalling them. Finally, anxious to salvage something out of these experiments, I began asking my dream acquaintances to tell me some information I could verify later, "just in case" they forgot the incident. Most of the details I obtained this way turned out to be accurate. Only a handful of dreams could be verified as mutual ones, but I did come across enough telepathic material to make it all worthwhile.

Here's a sample from one of those excursions:

I dream of meeting a man from school (a radio program host I had passed by several times at school without meeting). I know that I'm dreaming and that my lucidity may not last, so I corner him and ask him to give me something I can check out when I awaken. "I'd like to help," he says, "but I can't remember much of that (the waking state) right now."

"Well, what's the last thing you do remember?" I ask, fishing for whatever he can get from any state. He tells me his previous dream which, I hope, will be good for something.

In the dream, he says, he was hard at work writing a book; he planned to finish it by the summer. A house on a hill overlooking the ocean formed his dream environment, presumably his home.

Right after telling me his dream he leaves. I repeat the details of the dream to myself several times and then, feeling my lucidity start to fade, I wake myself up.

Though I had no previous desire to meet Michael T.,[7] my dream about him made a pretty good excuse. Several days later I spotted him standing in the hallway of the school. I walked over, introduced both myself and my interest in dreams, and said that I'd had a dream about him which I wanted to check out, just for curiosity's sake. He looked a bit stunned as I unraveled the plot, but waited for me to finish. Then he confirmed that, in the waking state, he lived in a house "on a hill overlooking the ocean," and that he was writing two books. He couldn't place the summer "deadline," but the other material seemed striking enough. We promised to meet again to discuss dreams. His bemused expression remained as we parted. "Very strange, very strange," he muttered to no one in particular as he walked away.

After a few weeks of adventures such as this, a new twist came up. I would dream about certain individuals while retaining full lucidity, and they would give me information about themselves which I planned to verify during the next several days. But then, later in the night, the person I had met would reappear, go over what he or she had told me, and correct it for accuracy! These return visits came suddenly and without any conscious intent on my part to evoke them. Whenever they happened, the resulting "improved" version turned out to be completely accurate.

The "Psychic Aura"

Psychics are fond of referring to the "aura" as the source of many of their psychic impressions. "Aura

---

[7] I believe I didn't learn his name until after we met, but I may have overheard someone mention it earlier.

reading'' has become a booming business, as have complicated courses for ''teaching'' the capacity to see the aura. All this fits so comfortably with the popular, show business side of paranormal matters, that many researchers are content to consider the ''aura'' a fraud and leave it alone. When Kirlian photography hit the media, it looked for a moment like some scientific back-up for the aura was on the way, but it soon became evident that the two were miles apart. Whatever it is that Kirlian photographs show, it is not the human aura. To the practiced viewer, the human aura appears to surround the entire body, and to extend at least three feet out. The great majority of auric activity takes place beyond the few millimeters of space which Kirlian photography records.

Those who can see the aura, perceive it as a combination of swirling shapes and colors which envelop an organism, or even an inanimate object. Everything has its own, unique aura, according to these perceivers. When seen clearly, auric colors seem incredibly bright, even opaque. The intensity of colors in the aura, the various shapes which make it up, and the particular hues of which it is composed, are in constant motion and are thought to represent the physical and emotional make-up of the being observed.

Although I have not pursued the art of seeing auras to a great extent, I do know ''how'' to see them and have taught others to do the same. The whole teaching process need not take more than ten to twenty minutes, by the way. Learning the technique is easy, applying it takes time and patience, and like so many things in this field, knowledge of a workable technique does not guarantee success. A simple method consists of looking for a slight haze surrounding the head of the person closest to you. As the haze comes into the visual field, you relax and try to let the haze extend further than the initial few inches. Then you allow colors to come in, and so on.

In classes where we've experimented with observing the aura of one selected subject, class members have come up with an unusual uniformity in the perception of specific colors and shapes. Whether this would hold for other groups I don't know. I do think that this would be something experimenters might follow up, whether with trained or untrained aura readers.

Anyway, even if the perception of the aura is roughly the same among psychics who see it, the interpretations are usually different, and often, so are the readers' definitions of what the aura is. My own opinion is that the aura is an imaginative translation (into visual form) of intuitive perceptions—a convenient vehicle for intuition, much like the "second body"[8] people use in OOB's. If this is so, then the aura need not have a measurable, physiological basis. My interpretation might help explain why some people can see color auras even when their subject is on black and white television. My opinion would not explain why the people in my classes saw the same forms and colors, nor would it negate that fact.

The best way to determine what is possible with aura viewing is to experiment with a gifted percipient. Fortunately, I have access to one. Pam Yellen, my companion on many journeys, has developed her auric sight as greatly as any person I know.

One of Pam's experiments in viewing auras took place when an acquaintance arranged for three people to meet Pam, for the specific purpose of observing her psychic sight in action. The people participating were a man, his 14 year old son and one of his son's friends. Pam describes the results as follows:

I looked at the older man's aura first. I noticed immediately that his aura was weak on his entire right side, though I could tell intuitively that he was right-handed. I told him that I felt his right side was

[8]See the glossary entry for "out-of-the-body experience" for more remarks on the "second body."

considerably weaker than his left, though I didn't know why, and that he seemed to be right-handed, nevertheless.

Then I watched the aura of his son's friend. There were dark spots which varied in shape and shade around his neck and head. I told him that I could see he had frequent headaches and a persistent ringing in his ears, and that both were the result of an injury to his neck a few years before.

The older man's son had an aura which shimmered in an unusual way. It also seemed somewhat retracted. There was a lot of activity around his hands. I told him what I could feel from this: that he was shy and preferred to be by himself, that he wasn't interested in academic pursuits in school, that he liked working with his hands and that his passion was electronics.

The older man, Thomas, confirmed that his right side was considerably weaker than the left and added that this was so because of an injury he received during World War II. He was right-handed.

Bill, the friend of Tom's son, verified my impressions of both his frequent headaches and the ringing in his ears. He said that, as I had mentioned, the two symptoms originated from a neck injury several years ago.

Tom's son Paul admitted his shyness, his disinterest in schoolwork, his appreciation for all kinds of work with his hands, and his complete fascination with electronics.

I did not witness this experiment, but I did speak with the man who arranged it. He assured me that Pam had read the auras as accurately as she claimed. He had no vested interest in the experiment's success. His confirmation came without any questioning on my part. More important, Pam has demonstrated her honesty to my complete satisfaction over the years I have known her. I have had quite a bit of experience firsthand with her aura viewing and its often startling precision.

One of the intriguing questions about seeing auras is:

How does the percipient get from the raw perceptual data of colors, patterns and shapes to the information itself? Although there are methods for interpreting auras which are taught by "aura readers," many are of dubious validity. There are also systems of aura reading described in the occult literature, but they consist mostly of psychological comments about the subject's "spiritual" development. Yet some also contain remarks about interpreting visual symbols which may appear super-imposed upon the aura itself. None that I know of describe such specific interpretations as a "ringing in the ears caused by injury to the neck," or some of the other equally detailed comments Pam gave.

I asked Pam for her thoughts about it all, including her opinion of the various interpretation systems available. This is how she responded:

I think that the information and the aura are things that you have to match up intuitively. I'm familiar with a number of systems for interpreting the aura, and I agree with them on a few points, but I think that it's better, in general, to throw out these systems. They're laden with the personal biases of the system's originator and they are too rigid—they don't allow for the fact that the aura is constantly changing.

One of the best ways to test out the validity of your interpretation is to work with a partner. Ask him or her to try to evoke a series of thoughts, feelings or states of consciousness while you observe the aura. Then tell your subject what changes you observed and what you think they signified. See how these observations correlate with whatever your partner experienced.

Some things I might look for in a quick viewing of the aura are the intensity and brilliance of the colors, which tell me the level of vitality of the person. The colors which make up the aura and the extent of the brilliancy are indications of a person's state of consciousness. If a person happens to be in a deep state of concentration or meditation, for example, this will show clearly. Grey or black spots point out painful and/or diseased places in the body.

I want to stress that these are ways in which I interpret the aura. Another person may perceive and interpret it in other ways.

Pam seems particularly talented at locating sites of pain in the body, by observing the "dark spots" mentioned above. This kind of work usually requires less complex forms of aura interpretation. It's often merely a matter of seeing the dark spots and pointing out the corresponding parts of the body. Places where the aura appears "weak" also figure in the physical well-being of the person, as Pam sees it. These correspond to places on the body which the person experiences as stressed or as more vulnerable.

My observations of aura interpretation at work suggest that talented readers could be a significant asset to the healing arts. Dr. C. Norman Shealy, a neurosurgeon who has held professorships in neurosurgery at the University of Wisconsin and the University of Minnesota, agrees.[9] He has used psychics for diagnostic assistance in his own medical work, and claims that their accuracy equals that of a competent physician. Not all "psychics" would be so capable, of course, but those who are could be identified by experiment, and used in conjunction with conventional medical assistance.

Moving Out-of-the-Body

I am lying in bed, having awakened in the middle of the night. Although I don't feel particularly relaxed, I decide

[9]C. Norman Shealy with Arthur Freese, *Occult Medicine Can Save Your Life* (New York: Bantam, 1975), pp. 43-44, 61-63, 216-225. The kind of medicine discussed in this book would be better labeled "alternative" instead of "occult," as Dr. Shealy includes autogenic training, biofeedback, electrical stimulation and other techniques in addition to psychic diagnosis.

to try an out-of-body induction anyway. I focus upon the tactile sensations in my arms and imagine a second set of non-physical arms within the physical ones. I imagine what it feels like to have these non-physical arms gently floating upward, without effort. My mental focus is interrupted repeatedly by fragmented thoughts and images, but I hold to the exercise.

Finally, after what seems like ten minutes, I feel my ''arms'' begin to rise. The temptation at this point is to try to move them too soon. I realize that if I do that, I will move my physical arms instead. So I keep still and relax into the upward movement. Within a minute, I feel my ''arms'' are above my chest. I have my eyes closed. The sensation of my arms above me is so similar to physical sensation that I wonder if I've mistakenly raised my physical arms. It seems that opening my eyes might disrupt the experiment.

Suddenly, the answer to the problem strikes me. I decide to see if I can pass my arms through each other. If so, then they are clearly non-physical. My arms meet at the wrists, solid and impermeable. For a second, I think I made a mistake somewhere. Then I relax and my arms go through each other, all resistance gone.

The next step is to get out-of-the-body entirely. I wave my ''arms'' around, grabbing for something to pull myself out with, and before long I'm back in normal body consciousness again. I chalk it up as a partial success.

When you are trying to get out-of-body, as I was in the above experiment, it seems like that in itself is the major hurdle. Once you are out, though, supposing that you have figured out where you want to go next (which is no easier a task out-of-the-body than in it), you have to learn to move where you want in the out-of-body frame of reference. Here's an example from Pam on that problem:

I started out in a dream which turned into a nightmare chase scene. In the midst of it I realized I didn't have to continue in the nightmare, that I could do what I want. I became fully lucid. The dream location remained and I decided to use it as a platform to go out-of-body. The thought of visiting my sister came to mind. This project had occupied me lately in out-of-body experiments, since I wanted to visit her and since I had never seen her apartment, nor heard any description of it. Her place seemed like a perfect location for getting some out-of-body information which could be verified.

I jumped off the dream ground, became a point of consciousness in the process, and felt myself whizzing through space at accelerating speed for a few seconds. Then I suddenly "crash-landed." I literally regained my senses to find myself lying at the foot of a bed. "Fantastic!" I thought. "I'm in her apartment!" But as I looked around, I discovered that I had actually landed at the foot of my own bed. My gaze faced the wall directly across the room from my bed. And on the wall were photographs of my sister! I'd wanted to see her, but this wasn't what I had in mind.

A few moments later I was back in my body, on the bed this time, amused and frustrated by the ironies of the experience.

It is important to remember that the kind of OOB induction you decide to use will affect the experience. If you try raising your imagined, non-physical arms, as I did in the experiment mentioned earlier, you are setting yourself up for a classic kind of "second body" projection. My own experiences with such projections, along with the reports I have heard from others, make me think that the "second body" is merely a convenient imaginative construct, a means of organizing OOB perceptions in a familiar way. The important point is that OOB's can release the experimenter from any bodily form whatsoever, physical, "astral,"[10] or otherwise.

Some OOB experimenters leave their bodies in the form of a "point of consciousness," as Pam did in the previous account; others take off as a "sphere of awareness" or as a "second body." All these explorations can be called "discrete OOB's," to indicate that they involve the displacement of one's spatial sense to a position outside the physical body. In another kind of OOB, the subject's awareness simply expands outward, extending beyond normal body boundaries. The following report comes from one of my former graduate students, Chris Lenz:

I was standing on a ship quite late at night, about four in the morning, and the ship's engines were throbbing very, very slowly. It seemed as I was standing there, calmly looking over the seascape, that I was not lifted out, not pushed away, but that I just extended, so that I felt I was looking down on the whole ship. There was a feeling at the same time of a super-calmness, the kind that I knew I couldn't get into ordinarily. I felt definitely distant from the ship; I could see it down there and yet, at the same time, I was on it. I knew that the regular boundaries we think of, with all the sense perceptions coming in here, were broken. I was just everywhere at once, looking around, and extending quite far.

The definition of what constitutes an out-of-body experience cannot be precise because OOB's, like all paranormal events, form part of the unbroken continuum presented by all forms of the imagination, including the waking state. Some projectors, like Oliver Fox,[11] seem to

---

[10]Some experimenters and writers use the term "astral body" to refer to the "second body." By extension, these same people call OOB's "astral projections."

[11]Oliver Fox, *Astral Projection: A Record of Out-of-the-Body Experiences* (Secaucus, NJ: Citadel, 1962).

be describing lucid dreaming rather than OOB's. Robert Monroe reports similarly strange OOB's among his "Locale II" visits.[12] Another projector, Sylvan Muldoon,[13] appears to visit earth-like surroundings, almost exclusively, in his OOB excursions.

My own projections have been a mixture. In some cases I find myself hovering inside my house, but with a strange twist: key parts of the environment appear in mirror-relation to their waking state status. A lamp is on the right side of the bed, instead of its normal left side position, a door opens from the wall opposite to the usual one, and so on. Some of my OOB's seem to take place in an environment which exactly duplicates the waking state environment; the only major difference is the spatial perspective of my awareness. Other OOB's contain "distortions," unexplained variations within an environment that otherwise matches the waking state one. I also have still other projections, which involve locales quite unlike any I've encountered in the waking state.

If there is no need to assume the existence of an "astral body," then we can drop the idea of "astral planes" as well. The major reason for holding such unnecessary hypotheses is that they seem to give a solidity to OOB's which is not shared by daydreams, fantasies, hallucinations, and the range of other paranormal phenomena unacceptable to conventional thinking, except as second-rate distortions of the "real" waking state. The pseudo-validity generated by such concepts as the "astral body" can only be achieved at the cost of creating a rigid set of categories which will prove to be as confining as the categories which make up the everyday world (a world of thoughts), that adventurers need to escape.

[12]Robert Monroe, *Journeys Out of the Body* (Garden City, NY: Anchor, 1973).

[13]Sylvan Muldoon and Hereward Carrington, *The Projection of the Astral Body* (New York: Samuel Weiser, 1970).

"Validity" and "verifiability" are two different matters. The first term is, like the word "real," often a pretext for asserting the desirability of one's own set of preferences. A "valid" anything is a matter of opinion; a "verifiable" OOB is not. To check out an OOB (to my mind a better term than "verify"), the experimenter tries to extract paranormal information from the experience. Various questions are asked: Did the projector observe exactly the same environment a physical observer in the OOB location would have? What did the projector know about the visited location prior to going there out-of-body?

One goal of paranormal perception is to get incoming information to bypass the usual channels. Yet, although alternative perceptions of all kinds are available, very few of them qualify as paranormal. To learn to perceive paranormally is a great art, as great as learning to perceive in the normal fashion, which we take so much for granted. Even more fantastic is the fact that there is always more to perceive and more ways to perceive it.

Waking/Dream Exchanges

Years ago I had a dream experience which jolted me out of the normal waking state/dream state dichotomy. Here's the dream and its aftermath:

After an exhausting night of meditative experiments, I collapse on the bed of my college room and fall asleep immediately. Soon I begin an extremely prosaic dream: I am in the school's student center observing David P. talk on the telephone. David seems to be talking to a lawyer about his draft-law difficulties. (David is trying for conscientious objector status.) José X. is sitting by the large plate glass window opposite the desk phone, and is obviously paying close attention to David's conversation. After a few minutes of this I wake up.

The amazing dullness of the dream plot attracts my

waking attention. I begin to wonder whether or not the dream reflects any waking state situation in progress. I go over the central elements of the dream, which is easy since they are few, note the time of the dream (11:30 a.m.), get up, dress and go out to check the details.

I meet José several hours later and stop him. "You know, it's odd, but I wonder if you could help me out with something. Were you in the student center this morning, watching David P. on the phone about his draft status?"

"Yeah, sure," says José. "So what?"

"When did it happen?" I ask.

"Between 11 and 12," he replies.

"My God, I dreamed it! I dreamed all of it!" My enthusiasm is getting the best of me about now and José looks like he's witnessing a classic psychosis in action.

"You must have been there," he mutters. "Maybe you just don't remember."

"I was asleep all this morning," I insist, knowing he won't believe me. "I didn't get up until noon." Sure enough, he doesn't believe it. He mumbles some variation on his first "explanation" and I walk off.

Two things impressed me a great deal: first, that my dream and the waking state event coincided in time, at least closely; and second, the ordinary, even dull quality of the dream experience itself. During the dream I felt exactly as if I was awake—I had no particular interest in what was going on in the student center, but having nothing better to do, I paid mild attention anyway. In short, I had experienced the whole thing as if I had actually been there. Only, space/time lines seemed to have crossed somewhere, since José had not seen me there, and from my point of view, I had been asleep the whole time. What was going on?

I concluded that, normal Aristotelian logic aside, I had both been there and been dreaming at the same time. The parapsychological "explanation" of the event as a kind of super-telepathic dream just didn't hold water when I remembered the complete conviction of waking state status I had felt in the dream. My memory of the dream events had the impact and verifiability of any waking state memory. The absence of dream "distortion" made me think that "dream telepathy" was too weak an explanation for what had happened.

Since then, I have learned to be more flexible in my approach to dreams and have tried to let dream experiences dictate my theories rather than the other way around. One major conclusion I retain from that experience some years back is that "dreaming" and "waking" are not the separate, airtight compartments conventional thinking would indicate. This conclusion broadened my appreciation of dreaming, but it also expanded my view of the "waking state." Later paranormal and altered state experiences convinced me that the "waking state" wasn't as solid and inflexible as I had previously thought. Paranormal acts, like other singularities, demonstrate that flexibility.

I have found myself in the midst of numerous waking/dream exchanges since the one described above, particularly in the context of seminars, workshops and graduate school classes I conduct on some of the frontier edges of the study of consciousness. This kind of interesting experience has come up outside of class settings, too. Here is an example:

Pam Yellen and I were separated by a significant geographical distance. We were planning to meet again upon her return to the city where we lived. Earlier, the two of us had tried our luck at psychometry experiments. Each of us would do a brief ink drawing in such a way that neither of us could see the other's paper, pen, etc. We would then fold up the paper a number of times, meet and exchange the folded papers, and holding them inside of a closed hand, try to figure out the drawing. I didn't do so well at this, making only occasional "hits," but Pam did very well, often to the point of being able to duplicate my drawing with all the essential details included.

While she was away, I felt the urge to do a pen and ink drawing, much like I would if we were to try a psychometry experiment. The thought crossed my mind that I might see if Pam could figure it out at a later time. I waited for awhile, trying to think of a picture with different elements from any previous ones I had drawn. Finally, I drew the outline of a mountain. On the top of the mountain came a circle of people with arms intertwined. In the midst of the circle lay a baby. The theme seemed unusual, but had no particular emotional impact upon me. I set it aside. It was the only drawing I did during the time.

Pam returned with the memory of an unusual dream that she wanted to tell me. "I dreamt that I was part of a group performing a dance ritual. The ceremony was a very significant part of our culture. Anyway, in it we danced in a circle around this baby. All of us were on a mountain top."

"Great!" I said. Then I told her about my drawing. We checked dates and discovered that I had drawn the scene on the evening she dreamt it.

Pam's dream and my drawing fall more easily into either the classical "telepathy" or "synchronicity" paradigms than does my previous dream visit to the college student center. But I'm not even sure that slotting paranormal experiences into one or more paradigms is all that useful, though it's certainly an addictive occupation for anyone (including myself, at times) who enjoys spinning out theories. I think that more interesting results come from looking through the holes of any given paradigm, including paradigms created on the spot by the puzzled researcher. What I am talking about here applies to the poetic, psychological and experiential approaches to the study of consciousness—the approaches which I prefer. But it has meaning for the natural sciences as well. A remark from Iris Owen and Margaret Sparrow, the authors of *Conjuring Up Philip: An Experiment in*

Psychokinesis (New York: Pocket Books, 1977, pp. 50-51), expresses this thought:

> It often happens in the field of parapsychological research, as indeed in other disciplines, that investigators are so intent on their own line of thinking, on the results they are hoping to produce, that they ignore other profitable and equally interesting side effects that might come their way. . . Such an attitude reminds one of the ''shaggy dog'' story of the milkman's horse. A man going along the street one day was addressed by a dejected-looking horse, pulling a wagon. ''Say,'' said the horse, ''do you know, only a couple of years ago I won the Grand National, and now look at me, pulling this wagon, and at the beck and call of a little man shouting 'Go' and 'Whoa!' '' The bystander, greatly amazed at being addressed by a horse, stopped the milkman as he emerged carrying his bottles from a nearby apartment house. ''Do you know your horse can talk? He has just told me he won the Grand National! What a remarkable animal!'' ''Take no notice of him,'' replied the milkman. ''He never won the Grand National; he was thirteenth. He tells everyone that he came in first.''[14]

I try to help my students avoid the milkman's rigidity of outlook by pointing out that terms like ''out-of-the-body experience,'' ''lucid dreaming,'' ''mutual dreams,'' and so on, are ''field'' phrases, meant primarily to introduce the explorer to new types of experience. Otherwise, I get people who are so fascinated by already-defined kinds of paranormal or dream experience that they dismiss events which don't fit the new pigeonholes.

It always amazes me when people can say in a dream class, for example, that they had a lot of dreams during the week, but none of them interesting enough to talk

---

[14]It is possible to describe experiences and experiments precisely, from any of the approaches I mention here. The natural sciences have no monopoly on either precision or ambiguity.

about. How do they know? Some of my most vivid and accurate telepathic dreams were boring . . . until they checked out. There are gems in that "garbage." Yet, merely extending your interest to a few previously ignored realms of experience (mutual dreams, telepathy, synchronistic events, et al.), is not enough. All dreams are extraordinary, all are "nothing special." However, in my experience, if you can't hold both sides of that insight, then sticking to the first part is the best. And of course, instead of "dreams," you can substitute the word "experiences" with equal validity.

Class Experiments: Tuning In

In order to fully appreciate the strange things that can happen in a dream class, you need to realize first of all, that "dreams" are valid experiences in their own right, and secondly, that calling an experience a "dream" may tell you very little about it, other than its chronology, the fact that it happened at night, morning, or whenever it is you happen to enter the fantastic possibilities of "sleep."

Some of the most interesting dream/waking crossovers happen when one class member tunes into another repeatedly, with verifiable results. What factors mediate this possibility cannot be definitively established for all cases. Anything that interests you in another person can count as a help in telepathic experiments, whether that interest arises from sexual attraction, intellectual curiosity, or an established personal relationship. The same holds for waking/dream exchanges, a category which I feel goes beyond "dream telepathy," for reasons I've already given. However, simple psychodynamic processes are not the whole story, since the paranormal can operate with two or more people who do not connect in the usual emotional ways. Psychics usually refer to such cases as ones of mutual "psychic receptivity," which doesn't explain much but isn't bad as a convenient catch-all. On occasion, the phrase also describes the feeling of the participants, which makes "receptivity" a little more meaningful as a description than one might think.

The following series involved Pam Yellen and Tom W. and occurred during a graduate dream class I taught in spring, 1977. The three exchanges took place over a little more than two weeks' time. Although I watched the adventure unfold, I'll let Pam tell the story.

One morning I dreamt that Jim and I were hiking along a dry riverbed in a hilly area with dry brush. A couple followed a few steps behind us. I knew that they were behind us, but not who they were, though the rest of the dream was particularly vivid.

The dream class which I attended met each week, so at the next meeting I mentioned the dream to the class. Tom W., amazed by the dream, asked me if I had recorded the exact time of the dream. "Yes, it was 10 a.m., April 13," I responded.

"This is mind-blowing," Tom replied. "At that exact time I was walking along a dry river-bed, in the kind of country you described, with my wife!"

It seemed that Tom and his wife were the couple behind Jim and I in the dream! Only, they didn't remember our presence there. Tom did mention later that the scene seemed particularly vivid to him at the time.

One aspect of Pam's dream which often pops up in mutual dreams and waking/dream exchanges is the fuzziness of her recall of the couple walking behind her. In many of the mutual dreams which I have seen validated in my classes, the dreamer's companion(s) appeared indistinct. Since beginning students often have no idea whether or not a dream is mutual, telepathic, or otherwise paranormal or not, prior to telling it in class, I have them recount a good deal of their dream content. Eventually, some get the ability to distinguish paranormal dream events prospectively rather than retrospectively, but even these students miss on occasion.

The next dream in the series shared the specific

"indistinctness" of the previous one. Again, here is Pam's description:

A week after my first dream involving Tom's waking state I had another. In it, I dreamt of leaving on an airplane ride with two other people, a man and a woman. I decided not to sit with them and moved to another section of the plane.

Upon awakening, I felt the dream concerned someone in the dream class, probably Tom. During the next class I mentioned the dream, looking directly at Tom as I did so, and asked if anything about the dream checked out. "Well, you've done it again," he said. He continued to say that on the day of my dream he had gone on a plane ride with a woman in the waking state.

The third and final dream of the series contained a new twist: a combination of waking/dream exchange and mutual dream content. Here it is:

On the morning of April 29, I dream of being with a group of people at a beach. I notice some kids jumping and playing in a part of the ocean that looks rocky and dangerous to me. The beach is familiar, one I've visited in the waking state, north of Santa Cruz. To show me that the kids aren't in danger after all, the water obligingly disappears for a moment and I see a smooth surface beneath it. As soon as I awaken from the dream I notice the time: 11:00 a.m. This time I'm sure the dream has to do with Tom, and reflects something happening concurrently in his waking state.

When I mentioned the dream to Tom in the next dream class, he confirmed the waking part of our dream/waking combination. Not only had be been at the beach at 11 a.m. of the same morning, but he'd visited the same exact beach! There were kids playing around in his perception as well. But there was more. Earlier the same morning, Tom had dreamt of being at the beach during an earthquake. As the ground shook, the water suddenly receded, revealing the bottom as in my dream. To top it off, I had still another dream in my dream log, which had taken place just before the other beach one. In it I was walking with a group along a beach when the water suddenly receded.

It seems that Pam became more certain of the paranormal direction of her dreams as the series progressed. She felt certain that the last dream had to do with Tom, while she had no idea whom the first dream reflected.

When I asked Pam if she had any notion why she had picked Tom and not someone else for these exchanges, she said that she didn't know, but that it did seem easier to continue tuning into him once she had begun the process. She learned to recognize which dream of a given week related to Tom, and by the third dream of the series, even wrote a comment in her journal alongside the dream that it had been about him. And, at no time during the class did she inaccurately attribute one of her dreams to Tom's waking state.

Stranger Still

In another dream class which I taught, this one in 1976, Pam came up with some even ''curioser'' material, as Alice in Wonderland might say. I contributed a little to this particular experiment. Another member of the class, Gary W., contributed a lot more.

It all seemed to start with an experiment Pam and I conducted on a Sunday night, October 19. We decided that it would be interesting to see if we could convey a particular dream theme to the class as a whole, by telepathic means. The theme we chose: beach dreams.

Later that night, Pam had the following dream:

I am in the dream class and we are telling our dreams. Gary W. starts telling us beach dreams. He had one particularly intense one on Saturday night and another on

Sunday. One of them involved swimming. (During the class he tells details about the dreams, but I've forgotten them.) His dream from Saturday night is very powerful, at archetypal levels. Other class members also tell beach dreams, and Jim and I decide that our experiment was successful. We also think that Gary may have telepathically influenced us into choosing the beach as a class experiment topic.

A few nights before, Pam had dreamt about the beach with content that also turned out to be related to all of this. The dream went as follows:

On Thursday night I dream of being with a group of people at the beach. I am wearing a very interesting, magical ring, opalescent with colors that radiate and change as I watch them. I see a woman with a ring that is similar to mine. She has shoulder-length brown hair, and is in her late twenties or early thirties. I think she's being careless with her ring. I warn her to be careful, that she will definitely lose it otherwise.

In the dream class, we discovered that Gary had dreamt of being on the beach on Saturday night. In his dream he struggled with a woman who tried to wrest his favorite ring from him. Though he used as much strength as he could, she won out and fled with the prize. The following day, Sunday, in the *waking state*, Gary went to a beach, lost the ring and was unable to find it. Sunday evening was the night Pam and I had set up our "beach theme" experiment, and also the night Pam wondered (in her dream) whether Gary had telepathically influenced our choice of theme. Not only that, but Gary had written down Pam's name with a question mark beside it in his journal, to indicate that he thought Pam might have been the woman, though the dream lady didn't look all that similar to Pam physically.

The cap to the incident came when Gary pressed Pam for further description of the mystery woman in Pam's

Thursday night dream. Her description matched perfectly with what Gary could remember of the woman he battled in his dream! It seemed that Pam had seen the woman who stole Gary's ring (from his dream) *before* the event occurred in Gary's dream time. This, along with the disappearance of Gary's ring during his waking state, made for some very intriguing correspondences.

Experiences like these indicate the fascinating potentials of the dream state, without in the least limiting the horizon. Again, the question is not what "causes" such experiences, but what kinds of further explorations can be inspired by them. The question I will leave to interested readers, my students and myself. I don't anticipate any overcrowding of the field. When the world itself becomes the playground, how can there be room for anything less than everyone?

2

Stories
of
Transcendence

Joseph Chilton Pearce summarizes a significant key to his thinking in the chapter title of one of his books.[1] The title is: "Behold and Become." Pearce's point is that many adults have lost their childhood capacity to reach beyond the conventional set of expectations and logic which make up the experienced world. The key to regaining this lost openness is the realization of how "cracks in the cosmic egg" function: suspending the normal view of what is possible and then taking on a different set of assumptions allows the "impossible" to happen. This is the principle utilized by the firewalker, the psychic and even the physicist. The importance of the "behold and become" concept lies in the fact that creative possibilities are accelerated when people can "behold" them, that is, envision the reality of events previously believed inaccessible.

This is a key concept in a number of respects, particularly in regard to the paranormal. The "para-

<hr>

[1] Joseph Chilton Pearce, *The Crack in the Cosmic Egg* (New York: Pocket Books, 1971), p. 116.

normal'' is the name given to a certain set of known possibilities which, as yet, occur infrequently. Thus the label ''paranormal'' is just as limiting as what is implied by the word ''hypnosis''; each term refers to a specified subset of possibilities that are available to the reality-shaping function of the mind. That function can reach further, however, and it is a serious mistake to think that any study of the paranormal will find the limits of that function. The understanding I advocate here, that study of the paranormal be based upon breaking limits rather than inscribing new ones, is the fundamental reason for an approach to the paranormal which emphasizes creative imagination. Imagination provides the vision which can then be given form. The process of imagining is not limited to the confines of past experience, although the past is the foundation of rational thought. Openness to new possibilities and radical discontinuities transcends thought that is merely rational, and makes possible world-transformation.

Pearce says the following:

> . . . We seek and we find. What we find is up to us. We knock and the door opens to us. There are an unlimited number of doors. We choose some, even as we are born with others ajar and absorbing us into their interiors, whether we like it or not, or *know* it or not.[2]

Imagination is crucial to the process of allowing new possibilities to enter, including the paranormal. Though the vision of transcending limits may arise internally, it more frequently comes from outside, from ''hearing and believing,'' from *stories*. Myths provide world-continuity; they also provide the vision of possible new orders.

---

[2]Pearce, p. 82.

Conscious intent[3] involves a structuring of reality according to the dictates of vision. To the imagination all things are possible; which possibilities are actualized depends upon the structuring process.

Much paranormal experience is triggered by hearing of its occurrence in someone else. In attempting out-of-body experience, for example, the experimenter often finds that success comes after days of reading, thinking and fantasizing about the experience. The actual form of a paranormal or altered state event frequently depends upon the stories you have been told, your background expectation, even if those stories have been latent since childhood. The important thing to remember here is that whether the story is fictional or nonfictional, its power to shape experience remains.

An often neglected area of study for those interested in the paranormal is science fiction. The phrase, "science fiction," itself embodies the paradox and transformation implicit in inner development.[4] "Science," of all words, represents "reality" for many in our present culture; "fiction" points to the other side, to imagination, and the two together imply the synthesis which emerges when both are cultivated—not always a happy combination.

[3]The concept of "conscious intent" is an expansion of the idea of aware self-suggestion found in the literature on hypnosis. When a person employs conscious intent, he or she uses imagination and will (often in a receptive, relaxed and alert fashion), in order to directly affect psychological and/or physical processes.

[4]"Outer" and "inner" orders of experience interweave as precipitously as do "science" and "fiction"; chemicals induce spectacular changes in consciousness, conscious intent directly affects physical material, and so on. Differentiation is not a simple matter of separating "outer" and "inner" realities. Authors may cling to the dichotomy of "objectivity" and "subjectivity," magicians may warn against "mixing the planes," but it is much too late for such primitive strategies.

Negative, destructive themes dominate science fiction writing presently, but this may change.

Authors of contemporary fiction are beginning to take serious note of paranormal events, and in some cases such events form an integral part of novels in the cultural "mainstream." Science fiction writers have dealt with such possibilities for many years, however, now a different kind of literature has appeared, potentially more significant in terms of social consequences. This literature presents the vision of consciously structuring reality to many readers who may now give the idea a second chance.

Stories can influence the structuring of possibility, in either constricting or expanding directions. As Pearce points out, imaginative thinking itself has no value judgment; anything can be created.[5] A story may hinge upon either a positive or deleterious "miracle," a happy or tragic ending. This factor helps distinguish contemporary literary approaches from previous ones, the latter being almost exclusively tragic. Too often, participants in these fictional non-ordinary events meet bad ends. This in itself tells something of the cultural addiction to tragedy and the implicit message that transcendence is a dangerous, negative undertaking. Both the Faust and Christ stories come to mind as examples of this fearful kind of outlook.

In the following pages I will present examples from contemporary literature which provide visions of paranormal frontiers. Such a short study cannot be complete, but at least it can show some of the directions evolving out of the current literary interest in this area.

An early novel concerned with paranormal powers is *Odd John*,[6] written by Olaf Stapledon in 1936. The principal character is a kind of supernormal mutant whose intellectual and psychic powers are so far above the norm

[5]Pearce, p. 122.

[6]Olaf Stapledon, *Odd John* (New York: Dover, 1936).

that he feels little in common with "Homo Sapiens." He prefers to consider himself a member of a new species: "Homo Superior." Odd John, as he is called, displays these powers in a Nietzschean disregard for humanitarian concerns. He falls into manipulating people, more out of curiosity than anything else. Eventually, as he grows older, he searches telepathically for others of his own kind. He dedicates his subsequent activity towards creating a super-race. The parallels of this plot to the Aryan mythos of Nazism are painful and obvious, especially considering the time in which this novel appeared. At least Stapledon's characters, Odd John and his partners, display real super-powers, but the ethical gaps are the same.

Odd John bands others like him into a colony. The group ends up destroying itself before the rest of the world does, and I wonder if this is really such a bad outcome. The deficiency of the plot lies in the complete disregard these supernormals show toward their fellow human beings. To Stapledon's credit, the story's narrator questions Odd John on just this issue throughout the book, but John's answers are unsatisfactory. The basic point of view embodied in the story seems to be the corruption of power, a corruption intensified when the powers are immense. The supernormals engage themselves in a polarized struggle against the rest of humanity. The battle grows when they isolate themselves, both physically and psychologically, from everyone else.

There are some aspects of this story which are quite credible. Powers of the magnitude Stapledon portrays would generate difficulties in a world where political and military power struggles take precedence. The entire novel can be read as a warning against placing the paranormal in the context of Earth's territorial power-games, and as an enjoinder to those with paranormal abilities to feel compassion rather than contempt for their fellow humans. The problem with Odd John is that he defines his abilities in terms of alienation. He finds no better use for his skills than merely perpetuating the existence of people like himself, a variation on a theme played out by many people of only average intelligence and ability. His goal of world-transformation is reasonable enough, but not his chosen means of accomplishing this task. The content or expression of power is clearly as important as the fact of power itself.

In 1953, Arthur C. Clarke produced his science fiction novel, *Childhood's End*.[7] In it, Clarke describes the emergence of a new species with paranormal powers strong enough to radically alter matter. In Clarke's tale, the new children emerge after Earth is contacted by the Overlords, extraterrestrial visitants who appear to help the transition along. These Overlords direct the Earth into a kind of utopia through an inspired management that is authoritarian, but "for humanity's good." Eventually, the child prodigies start being born, exhibit their powers, and, in the process, initiate the next phase in evolution for humanity. This phase ends when the children dance the Earth into the sun, an act which merges their awareness with a superior intelligence named the "Overmind."

Clarke's story leaves the reader with a very vague idea of just what the evolutionary advancement consists of, though he does say it involves moving human identity beyond bodily matter. Like Stapledon, Clarke raises the issue of evolutionary development. Clarke associates the evolutionary movement with paranormal abilities. He also ends his story with an apocalypse, but in *Childhood's End*, the children supplant the rest of humanity instead of the other way around.

Another book from the 1950's, *The Midwich Cuckoos*,[8] became the base for two movies: "Village of the

---

[7]Arthur C. Clarke, *Childhood's End* (New York: Ballantine, 1953).

[8]John Wyndham, *The Midwich Cuckoos* (New York: Ballantine, 1957).

Damned'' and ''Children of the Damned.'' Despite the lurid film titles, the book belongs with others of archetypal and evolutionary thematic content, not with books in the horror genre. In the story, the appearance of UFO's heralds sudden and inexplicable pregnancies of women around the world. The children resulting from these pregnancies have golden eyes, psychic powers, super-intelligence, and an additional factor—a group mind. The author suggests that this group mind is the evolutionary development which allows for much of the paranormal and intellectual wizardry practiced by the children.

When one child of this group learns something, all of them learn it. The children present a familiar problem though; they show complete disregard for other people. The military-industrial faction shows alarm at the children's existence and finally destroys them. The story, like many of the genre, ends up showing a potentially positive evolutionary step in fearful, hostile terms. The author pictures paranormal abilities as tools of evolutionary warfare; he emphasizes the coercive aspects of the children's powers.

The above three books all emphasize the evolutionary interpretation of psychic abilities, that the paranormal represents one of the signs of evolutionary advance. The books also portray paranormal abilities as a potential threat to the world, both to those who have the abilities and those who do not. In fact, each time the mutant super-species emerges, it becomes isolated from the larger world culture and either annihilates, or is annihilated by, that culture.

The mythos of advanced mutants in conflict with the larger mass of humanity gained a great deal of support among young people around the world during the 1960's. The young identified with the isolated new species characterized in science fiction; feelings of alienation and persecution followed logically as the entire culture played out the script. These consequences could have been predicted merely by looking at the plots of the novels which exemplified and perhaps encouraged such views. It is hard to gauge the importance of any particular work in evoking this mythos. *Childhood's End*, by Clarke, was certainly popular, but so were a number of other books. Though the mythic themes of these other books are related to the "mutation" metaphor, a full discussion of them will have to be left to a larger writing on the subject.

There is one more book to be considered here which fits quite clearly into the category of science fiction: *The Three Stigmata of Palmer Eldritch*, by Philip K. Dick.[9] This book's subject differs considerably from the three novels mentioned earlier. To summarize rapidly: In this story, Palmer Eldritch is an advanced alien intelligence, having become so as a result of a trip to a strange planetary system. Eldritch brings back a new drug, called Chew Z, which moon colonists discover creates the capacity to project the ingester's consciousness into "real" pasts and futures, thus giving the experimenter hope of changing the present. The problem here is that every place the drug takers go, they find Eldritch already there. He has achieved one of the characteristics formerly attributed only to God—omnipresence. Eldritch tries to help people with their problem-solving in various time frames. The catch is that the more Eldritch acts to alter the circumstances of other people, the more he is projecting his identity into everything. Finally, persons who have taken Chew Z realize that everyone is turning into Palmer Eldritch.

There are other interesting sub-plots in the book, but these are too detailed to mention here. The basic ironic twist, though, is quite valid, and is an original warning to all would-be gods. Paranormal abilities are founded on the reality-structuring capability of the mind. If these powers are developed to the degree illustrated in Dick's novel,

9Philip K. Dick, *The Three Stigmata of Palmer Eldritch* (Middlesex, England: Penguin, 1964).

which seems unlikely, then people will have to take care to avoid projecting their waking personalities everywhere in a misguided attempt to improve the world.

The Education of Oversoul Seven,[10] by Jane Roberts, is a book which cannot fit easily into any of the ready categories for current fiction. The plot includes six major characters: Cyprus, Oversoul Seven, and Seven's incarnations: Ma-ah (35,000 B.C.), Josef (17th century), Lydia (20th century) and Proteus (2300 A.D.). Cyprus, Oversoul Seven's teacher, conducts an examination on the nature of being. Seven's ''education'' consists of answering the exam. Dreams, out-of-body experience, and reincarnational existence are major themes of the story, but the central one is that each individual creates his or her own reality. Seven's ''incarnations'' exist simultaneously, from the standpoint of Oversoul Seven, though they all experience a waking state world of linear, sequential time. Occasionally, their lives intersect in a mutual dream. A waking state event for Ma-ah—viewing the beautiful tiles in the courtyard of the Speakers—provides both inspiration for one of Josef's paintings and a paranormal vision of the past for Proteus.

Roberts shows paranormal abilities at work in a context which lies outside the traditional power-struggle motif. If her characters struggle, they do so for understanding, and the paranormal events which happen encourage that understanding. To the book's characters, the paranormal aspects of experience reveal something of the greater sense of meaning possible for those willing to look. Some parts of the story show practical and amusing applications for intuitive abilities. In one chapter, Lydia, incarcerated in a home for the aged, is taught out-of-body travel by her companion, Cromwell. *In* his body, Cromwell slurs his words, drools and generally acts like the ''senile'' person

[10]Jane Roberts, *The Education of Oversoul Seven* (Englewood Cliffs, NJ: Prentice-Hall, 1973).

the nurses expect. But *out* of his body, he is clear-headed and helpful. Lydia realizes, as Roberts must have, that a person's inability to perform normal functions does not mean that there is no identity or consciousness left.

In *The Mind Parasites*,[11] Colin Wilson describes the difficulties some experimenters encounter when they try to develop mental powers beyond ordinary human capacity. The following quote from the book illustrates Wilson's approach to the paranormal:

> The moment man stumbles on the fact that his attention is a 'beam',. . . he has learned the fundamental secret. Now all he has to learn is how to polarize that beam. It is the 'polarized' beam that exerts PK [psychokinetic] effects.[12]

In Wilson's novel, "mind parasites" attack the protagonists, sapping their sense of purpose and inducing severe depression. The "parasites" try everything in their power to prevent the experimenters from attaining the new abilities the experiments are designed to evoke. Throughout the story, Wilson uses the metaphor of the alien "mind parasites" in an attempt to map out the struggle human beings encounter when they volitionally transcend the "ordinary." Of course, in human life, the parasites are internal forces, not external beings, and Wilson discusses the problem of bypassing these obstacles in his nonfictional and fictional writings. Still, there is good reason to behave as though the parasites were, in a sense, external forces, while recognizing their true origin. A method of this kind allows detachment from the strictures of negative emotions, including boredom, which limit imaginative and psychic powers.

[11]Colin Wilson, *The Mind Parasites* (Oakland, CA: Oneiric Press, 1972).

[12]Wilson, p. 105.

One of the reasons why people tolerate a generalized lowering of vitality is that they identify with their negative emotional states. Although persons and events in the external environment may contribute to a lowered sense of energy, the major source is the internal habit of passivity. Wilson understands that paranormal abilities form part of what he calls "Faculty X,"[13] the focusing of attention which extends the human sense of meaningfulness. He believes that this faculty, which opens new psychological and paranormal horizons to the explorer, is a key to the further evolution of humanity.[14,15]

Two books remain to be considered here. Both are by Doris Lessing, an English novelist writing in the cultural mainstream of contemporary fiction. The first book, *Briefing for a Descent into Hell*,[16] charts one man's excursion into visionary experience, interpreted by others as insanity. The protagonist is a professor, found wandering about the streets of London, confused and mumbling, without identification. Psychiatrists examine him and then hold him in a hospital. From his talk, the doctors realize that he believes he is on a sea journey aboard a raft. These doctors' voices are auditory hallucinations to the professor. After all, he surmises, a long time without food or water can produce such tricks of the mind, especially out at sea. Lessing plays upon the relativity of such labels as "madness," here and

[13]Colin Wilson, *The Occult: A History* (New York: Random House, 1971), pp. 58-62, pp. 575-582.

[14]Wilson, p. 62, p. 582.

[15]My own discussion of "conscious intent," an extension of the concept of aware self-suggestion found in the literature of hypnosis, strongly parallels Colin Wilson's formulation of "Faculty X." See James J. Donahoe, *Dream Reality* (Oakland, CA: Bench Press, rev. ed., 1979), pp. 31-43, pp. 119-123.

[16]Doris Lessing, *Briefing for a Descent into Hell* (New York: Bantam, 1971).

elsewhere in her books.

The professor enters a realm of archetypal experience in which he "remembers" his training prior to incarnating on the planet. The incarnation is the "descent" referred to in the book's title; in a sense, the book is itself a "briefing" for the reader. Lessing reinterprets madness, perhaps as a result of her personal contact with "mad" people. In the following passage, the professor describes one of his "symptoms," a sense of urgency:

> "My sense of urgency is very simple," said the Professor. "I've remembered that much. It's because what I have to remember has to do with time running out. And that's what anxiety is, in a lot of people. They know they have to do something, they should be doing something else, not just living hand to mouth, putting paint on their faces and decorating their caves. . . —and so the mental hospitals are full and the chemists flourishing."
> "Would you like a sleeping pill, Professor?"
> "No thank you, Nurse."[17]

The professor's madness is symptomatic of his attempts to become more awake. These attempts involve an enhancement of his perceptual powers, which because of their vividness, would be labelled "hallucinatory" by his doctors. He sees emotional states in the form of colors and facial changes, for example. At times he also gains a kind of clairvoyant vision in which he watches a webwork of lines connecting the beings and events which comprise the planet. He perceives meanings previously obscure to him; he recognizes paranormal contacts with his friends.

In *The Four-Gated City*,[18] Lessing continues the theme of madness, but draws upon her historical knowledge of

[17]Lessing, p. 273.

[18]Doris Lessing, *The Four-Gated City* (New York: Bantam, 1969).

the U.S.A. McCarthy era's equivalent in England. The heroine, Martha Quest, while exploring madness, realizes that much of her problem is the ability to hear the thoughts of others, to perceive *too much* without being able to integrate it. Martha does learn to integrate her perceptions and to use the paranormal abilities that result, while Linda, Martha's "mad" friend, does not progress.

One of the unique qualities of the story is Lessing's ability to create living characters who experience the paranormal in a human, historical context. In some ways, this kind of presentation teaches readers more than science fiction can, because a more human, familiar environment forms the stage. Lessing understands the strong connection between paranormal perception and normal perceptions and emotions. When people screen out the paranormal, they risk losing access to a whole range of insights, feelings and possibilities.

Stories, Interpretations and Waking Reality

Stories in which the paranormal and self-development are major themes often center upon their protagonists' quest for greater knowledge and ability. It is interesting to notice how many of these stories end unhappily; Prometheus gets chained to a rock, Jesus is crucified, the mutants are destroyed by the army. In fact, it is difficult to think of more than a few stories, ancient or contemporary, which present this theme and end with a positive resolution.[19]

These unhappy endings seem to imply that self-transcendence is a hazardous and ultimately deadly undertaking, and this premise may influence the reader.

[19]Two such stories were discussed earlier: *The Education of Oversoul Seven* and *The Mind Parasites*.

Someone might argue that such a propagandistic effect is nonsense, that myths are all make-believe anyway and thus have no effect upon how people view the ''real'' world; but to the child and perhaps preconsciously to the adult, stories provide a key means of thinking out the consequences of specific behaviors and experiences. That thinking takes place regardless of whether the conclusions so reached are ''true'' or ''false.'' Stories exert enormous influence upon the organization of experience, particularly when the experience is an extraordinary one. Perhaps one of the best things people can do to hasten evolutionary progress is to create their own life-affirming, compassionate and optimistic stories of self-transcendence.

3

Mutual Dreams

**Breakthroughs in Dreaming:
A Quick Survey**

The existence of mutual dreams[1] contradicts the common notion that dreams are somehow less "real" and are consequently less worthwhile than waking state events. These dreams fulfill the generally held criteria for a "real" event; i.e., that it be perceptually coherent and intense, and that it be consensually verifiable. The capacity to distinguish between waking and dream memories retains obvious practical advantages, but discovering that this distinction can be maintained without downgrading experience in either state of consciousness, is one goal of mutual dream research.

The bias of present culture remains solidly on the side

[1] In a "mutual dream," two or more people share an identical dream environment. There are two types of mutual dreaming. In the first, two or more people have the same dream, but without each being present in the other's dream plot. In the second type, at least two people participate in the same dream and are aware of each other's presence.

of waking state events. Dreams, OOB's and many altered state experiences are reduced to the status of "imagination." These experiences *are* examples of imagination, but not the pallid meaning of the word in common usage. For psychology researchers to expand their conception of "imagination," they need to reevaluate the nature of psychological events, and the interrelationship of personal awareness and observable, waking state phenomena.

As students of consciousness recognized well before William James, many modalities of awareness are possible, each with its own potential events. Experimentation with phenomena like mutual dreams helps to show that altered state events deserve further consideration. The significance and rarity of mutual dream research make it important that some examples of that research be presented here.

A mutual dream is one of a number of different dream types. Since these types tend to blend into one another, it is important to clarify what they are, and place the mutual dream within the larger context of frontier dream research.

Contemporary dream studies suggest an initial classification of seven areas of dream work. Certain pioneer researchers are associated with these areas, as follows: Celia Green (see bibliography) and Frederik Van Eeden[2] on lucid dreams; Charles Tart[3] on high dreams; Montague Ullman, Stanley Krippner and Alan Vaughan[4]

---

[2]Frederik Van Eeden, "A Study of Dreams," *Altered States of Consciousness*, ed. Charles T. Tart (Garden City, NY: Anchor, 1969), pp. 147-160.

[3]Charles T. Tart, "The 'High' Dream: A New State of Consciousness," *Altered States of Consciousness*, ed. Charles Tart, pp. 171-176.

[4]Montague Ullman, Stanley Krippner and Alan Vaughan, *Dream Telepathy* (New York: Penguin, 1973).

on telepathic and precognitive dreams; Kilton Stewart[5] and Patricia Garfield[6] on creative dreaming; Ann Faraday[7] on psychotherapeutic dream interpretation; and myself[8] on mutual dreams.

Three of the above terms require additional elaboration. A "lucid" dream is one in which the dreamer knows he or she is dreaming as the dream takes place. "Lucid" in this sense refers to more than just a heightened sense of clarity within a dream. A "high" dream is one in which the dreamer moves into an ecstatic state of consciousness analogous to certain psychedelic experiences. "Creative" dreaming, in the formal sense used by Stewart and Garfield, refers to an increase in the ability to consciously direct and cooperate with a dream while it occurs, as well as working with it from the waking state after the dream has ended.

The dream categories listed above are distinct, yet they are not mutually exclusive. A mutual dream may be lucid, telepathic and even a high dream, all at the same time.

A dream can be mutual in one of two ways. The participants may dream of being together in the same dream environment. Or, in the second case, each dreamer does not experience the presence of any of those sharing the dream—each person has the same dream, but

[5]Kilton Stewart, "Dream Theory in Malaya," *Altered States of Consciousness*, ed. Charles T. Tart, pp. 161-170.

[6]Patricia Garfield, *Creative Dreaming* (New York: Simon & Schuster, 1974).

[7]Ann Faraday, *Dream Power* (New York: Berkeley Medallion, 1973).

[8]James J. Donahoe, *Dream Reality* (Oakland, CA: Bench Press, rev. ed., 1979).

separately, not as a group experience.[9]

Although it is possible for someone to have a mutual dream which the others involved subsequently forgot, only the memory of those others can confirm that the dream was indeed shared. This possibility makes it important that would-be mutual dreamers attempt to enhance their general dream recall.

Mutual Dreams Recognized: Early Research

The common dream environment sets apart the mutual dream from other dream types. Hornell and Ella B. Hart identified the mutual dream as a special category of psychic experience as early as 1933. This ground-breaking research appeared in an article section entitled "Reciprocal Dreams," in the *Proceedings of the Society for Psychical Research*.[10]

The Harts discovered authenticated reports of dreams with mutual content by combing the records of psychical research. These dreams varied from ones with partial sharing of content to fully developed mutual dreams.

The earliest example the Harts could find took place over 80 years ago. The Harts' report is an example of a

[9]A full "mutual dream" requires that the people involved share the identical dream plot and environment. Obviously, there are dreams in which some details are shared and not others. These would be examples of dreams with shared content. The more people remember of their dreams, the more the extent of any sharing of dream content will be evident. I think that people who choose to describe their experiences in this area can be most helpful if they distinguish between full mutual dreams and dreams with some shared content, and if they present clearly delineated dream reports.

[10]Hornell Hart and Ella B. Hart, "Visions and Apparitions Collectively and Reciprocally Perceived," Vol. 41, *Proceedings of the Society for Psychical Research* (New York: American Society for Psychical Research, 1932-1933), pp. 234-240.

good series of case studies. It includes each dreamer's experience backed by strong support for the authenticity of the accounts. Here is the earliest account they present:

In Elmira, N.Y., on 26 January 1892, between 2 and 3 a.m., Dr. Adele Gleason dreamed that she stood in a lonesome place in the dark woods, that great fear came over her, that the presence of her friend, J.R. Joslyn came to her and shook a tree by her, and that its leaves began to turn to flame. On the same night, at the same hour, Joslyn dreamed in another house in Elmira, that he found Dr. Gleason in a lonely wood after dark, apparently paralysed with fear, that he went to her side and shook a bush, when the falling leaves turned into flame. Both dreamers met, four days after the event, she mentioned having had a strange dream, but that he at once stopped her and related his own dream first, without suggestion from her. Dr. Hodgson made written inquiries and found that Dr. Gleason had made a record of the dream in her notebook the morning after it occurred, and before she saw Joslyn.[11]

The above two dreamers shared the same dream environment with the exception of one small detail. The bush in one dream is a tree in the other. The events in the dream were strongly emotional in tone and of immediate significance to the dreamers. As far as can be determined, the dream did not refer telepathically to waking state events, nor were the dreamers lucid; i.e., aware of dreaming while the dream occurred. Finally, the style of consciousness in the dream is a combination of visionary and normal waking state perception.

The following example from the Harts illustrates a different type of shared dream content:

On the night of 3 July 1916, a man found himself lying on the floor, feeling very ill, unable to move or to call for help. About 3:35 in the morning he managed to call the cook,

[11]Hart and Hart, p. 235.

saying, "Come quickly, I am very ill." The cook sent the housemaid for some whiskey; they poured some into his mouth and then, with difficulty, got him into bed. He revived a little and said, "I am feeling very ill. I think I am dying."

On this same night this man's brother-in-law dreamed very vividly that he saw him lying unconscious and ghastly on the floor. In the dream he lifted him with difficulty to the bed. He then tried unavailingly to get assistance. A woman promised to get some whiskey, but did not come back.

On this same night the daughter of this dreamer also dreamed that her uncle had said "I am very ill" and had left the room, that she then found him lying unconscious, and that neither she nor others were able to go to his assistance.

The two dreamers, the cook, and the physician who treated the sick man, all signed statements covering their experiences. The father told his dream to the daughter before she related hers. It was not until the following day that they obtained from the uncle the information corresponding to their dreams.[12]

There is an interesting fluidity of dream/waking state boundary involved in accounts like the one above. One person's waking state scene takes place as a dream for two others. Like the previous account cited, this one shows strongly emotional dream content.

Another mutual dream given by the Harts suggests an essential similarity between dreaming and the kind of out-of-body or visionary experience in which subjects seem to communicate with people no longer living:

In January 1901 (somewhere in America?), a man and his wife both dreamed that his mother (who was dead) came into the room and stood at the foot of the wife's bed. The wife's dream included hearing the mother say that the wife's mother would not live three months. The dreamers told each other at breakfast. The husband sent a written account two days later, and the wife replied to an inquiry that she had nothing to add and no change to make in the statement made

[12]Hart and Hart, p. 237.

by her husband. The wife's mother (who was 83 years old, and seriously ill at the time of the dream) actually died six months later.[13]

As these accounts illustrate, mutual dreams often involve emotionally significant material. The dreams can be extremely negative in tone, or positive to the point of being high or peak experiences. The negative quality of dream events, as in nightmares, can be created entirely by unjustified and unnecessary fear on the part of the dreamer. This last example from the Harts shows this:

On the night of 7-8 June 1925, in London, Theodore Besterman dreamed that he was in a room with an elderly woman and two men. He was aware that the woman suffered from devil-seeing delusions. She thought he was a devil, and charged at him, full tilt. The two men held her back, but she seemed at the point of breaking loose. He then dreamed that he fainted because her movements and features became so horrible. When he recovered from the swoon, he was in icy terror, but at this point he was awakened by the screams of his wife. She had just been dreaming that she was with men friends visiting other people. She became convinced that one man, with a black eye, was a devil. Friends, who were standing behind her, urged her to sing a song, in which she pointed him out as a devil. His eyes then blazed up horribly and he seemed about to descend on her. She awoke screaming. Mr. and Mrs. Besterman each wrote out their own account of the dreams on the following day.[14]

Experimentation with lucid and creative dreaming has shown that nightmares can be changed from within the dream.[15] The opportunity for lucid dream work, together with the occurrence of mutual dreams, suggests another

[13]Hart and Hart, p. 236.

[14]Hart and Hart, p. 238.

[15]For a clear example of the lucid transformation of a nightmare, see Donahoe, p. 115.

possibility, that of one dreamer helping another from within the dream state. This particular kind of dream work could take many forms, among them psychotherapeutic assistance and even mutual experimentation with the dream state conducted from inside it. I provide an example of the latter mutual dream application later on in this chapter. In the dream, Pam watches what happens to my appearance as I wake myself up.

The Harts' work on mutual dreams consisted of collecting various mutual dream accounts. I take a more direct approach in my own work by attempting to elicit mutual dreams experimentally. When successful, this method both increases the sample of mutual dreams to be studied and allows for direct confirmation of the validity of the reports.

Seminars which concentrate upon dream and paranormal experience have a great advantage in the study of mutual dreams, as (1) participants are looking for the appearance of paranormal dream material and, (2) dream records can be brought to the seminar in order to verify shared dream content. This second advantage is an important one, particularly since a mutual dream may seem totally ''ordinary,'' with nothing to indicate that the dream was shared. Thus, mutual dream discoveries can occur unexpectedly during the course of a seminar meeting itself, as participants relate dreams from their journals.

Experiments in Mutual Dreamscapes

From March through June of 1974, I taught a class on the intentional use of the dream state at the California Institute of Asian Studies, a graduate school in San Francisco, California.[16] The students recorded their

[16]Research compiled principally from this class appeared in: James J. Donahoe, ''Exploring Mutual Dreaming,'' *Psychic Magazine*, December, 1975, pp. 23-25. Material from that article is included here in revised form.

dreams at home, then brought their dream journals in for verification of telepathic and mutual dream content. The class used various techniques to attempt to induce shared dream content, including pre-sleep conscious intent.[17] One of the interesting results was the frequency of paranormal exchange involving people who did not see each other outside of class. Researchers would suspect that shared dreams would be most common among people who knew each other well, and the class did seem to confirm this. But there were a number of telepathic and mutual dream instances which took place among students who were only slightly acquainted. Clearly, close interpersonal bonds can help in bringing about these dreams, but they are not a prerequisite.

One instance of a mutual dream involved two students, Pam Yellen and David:

David dreamed of walking on the beach, his attention drawn to the piles of intricate shells at his feet. A short time later he, his wife, and some friends played knee-deep in the water.

Pam also dreamed of walking on a beach which seemed unusual for its large amount of beautiful shells. She watched David standing in the ocean with some other people, one of whom she felt to be David's wife, Lynn. Although she had not met Lynn in the waking state, Pam now saw her vividly and accurately.

As Pam told her dream to the class she wavered on the description of Lynn's hair. "In the dream I saw her with light brown, long and straight hair, but now it seems she has a short, layered cut." David replied that at the time of the dream Lynn did have long hair, but that she had

[17]For further references on intentionally affecting dream content from the position of the waking state, see: Donahoe, pp. 45-65 and Charles Tart, "Toward the Experimental Control of Dreaming: A Review of the Literature," *Altered States of Consciousness*, pp. 134-146.

changed to a short shag cut a few days later. Both David and Pam had their dreams the same night.

Similar reports of telepathic and mutual dream experiences came from a number of students. Those who had them realized that such dreams really do happen, but not everyone was convinced. One student, Phil, expressed strong scepticism about the whole subject, even after hearing the reports of his classmates. He was willing to experiment by telling his dreams to people who had appeared in them, but he doubted anything would come of it. Then one day Phil came to class with an unusual story.

Phil told the class that he dreamt of walking alongside a road with a young woman he did not know in the waking state. As they walked he noticed snow-capped mountains in the distance. They decided to hitchhike, and soon after, along came one of Phil's friends, Susie, driving a blue Chevrolet. Susie stopped to pick them up and they drove away in silence. There was some emotional awkwardness about the situation, which he felt Susie could perceive.

A day after the dream, Phil saw Susie. He began to tell her the dream, just getting to the part where Susie came by, when Susie cut in, ''Yes, I was driving my blue Chevy, it was in Colorado, and I stopped for you.'' She had experienced the dream also, and she went on to recall additional details which Phil had forgotten. Phil was astonished, of course, particularly since Susie was not one of the members of the dream class.

Mutual dreams of this type resemble waking state experience in several important ways. Events can be verified consensually for both the mutual dream and for the waking state. Perceptual intensity and coherency, and consistency of plot are the same for both. This paradox, the existence of a dream having the qualities of a valid, waking state experience, certainly provides fertile ground for thought. But further discoveries along this line require adding more exploration and reports to those just presented.

Mutual dream content does not always coincide in every detail. At one meeting the class discovered that three of its members dreamed of seeing letters in an unknown language. The letters appeared in a type of crossword puzzle, grid pattern. The grid pattern occurred in more than one dream for some of the dreamers. In each of these "hieroglyph dreams," the dreamer attempted to translate the characters. Two of the dreamers remembered identical characters, having drawn them in their journals. The third verbally confirmed having seen the same ones. Two dreamed this the same night, the third experienced it a different night that week.

Those who dreamed of decoding the alien letters could think of no particular reason why this theme should show up. They could not recall any waking state stimulus which might have served as the foundation for the dream.[18]

Apparently none of the cases the Harts reported involved deliberate attempts to produce shared dreaming. Such reliance upon spontaneous cases of mutual dreams may be why the research in this area is so scarce. That research and reports of mutual dreams *are* scarce is indicated by the records kept by the Foundation for Research on the Nature of Man, located in Durham, North Carolina. The foundation maintains a file of thousands of paranormal dreams reported by the percipients. According to Mrs. J.B. Rhine, mutual dreams are reported so rarely that there is no separate file for them. Even those accounts that do arrive, she says, are hardly impressive enough to be fairly called shared dreams.[19]

[18]For the purpose of class discussion and experimentation, I defined a telepathic dream as one containing paranormal information about the *waking state* of someone other than the dreamer. We referred to the alien letters as mutual rather than telepathic dream content.

[19]Information on the foundation's files comes from correspondence between Mrs. J.B. Rhine and myself.

If mutual dreams are so rare, why did they occur so readily to members of my graduate class? It is doubtful that the reason lies in some unusual degree of psychic ability which class members shared. It was not because of previous experience with mutual dreams; most had never experienced them before.

Mutual dreams are not purely a matter of innate talent nor are they just inexplicable anomalies. The class simply learned that if they concentrated upon finding such dreams, the search would succeed much more often than might be expected.

Generating mutual dreams, like most psychic phenomena, does not seem to be a simple matter of turning the process on and off at will. The class provided a conducive environment for verifying shared dreams. Two factors, wanting to discover mutual dreams and attempting to verify potential ones, seemed to have the greatest effect upon producing them.

In many mutual dreams, two or more people experience being present in the same dream environment; they are aware of each other's presence while the dream goes on. However, one of my early mutual dreams did not involve this kind of sharing. In it, another person and I had the same dream, but each of us did not appear in the other's dream plot.

My version of the dream took the following form:

I found myself in the presence of a female guide figure. She told me that during the night I would have the opportunity to experience transcendent consciousness. A short time elapsed and suddenly I was in the presence of a male guide.

He said, "To get anything you have to give up something. To obtain everything you have to give up yourself." He held out a velvet pillow on which two jewelled daggers were placed. I took one, obviously offered for my self-annihilation, and wondered what to do. Perhaps it was a test, I reasoned, the right move being to reject the offer. I threw the dagger onto the ground.

The guide smiled and replied, "If you won't kill yourself, kill me." I refused. He picked up the remaining dagger and stabbed himself in the chest. His head rolled back and a sentence flashed on my inner screen, "He tasted bliss beyond words."

The guide opened his eyes and said, "Let's see what's happened here." He unbuttoned his shirt and on his chest was one tear-shaped drop, part blood, part water. The scene changed.

In the next instant I was walking towards the boarding ramp of an airplane. Last minute thoughts ran through my mind. I wondered if I had lost my chance and if so, how long it would be before I got another. As I stepped onto the ramp, the dream dissolved.

Pam's dream began with her encountering the male guide. Her experiences with the guide matched my account exactly. She met alone with him. She even saw the printed sentence describing the guide's "death."

Like the first example quoted from the Harts, this mutual dream was discovered by accident. Pam dreamed it while on vacation several hundred miles from the city where both of us lived. She found the dream interesting for its archetypal quality, and began telling it to me for the same reason. Once she realized that this had been a mutual dream, she was able to confirm that she experienced it on the same night as I. Each of us had recorded the dream in our personal journals.

This dream provided convincing evidence that daytime sensory experience could not account for mutual dream events. In the above case, neither Pam nor I could recall reading or thinking along lines even remotely similar to those of the dream. The event did show that archetypal dreams can be shared just as fully as comparatively ordinary ones.

Pam and I had another archetypal dream with mutual content, but with a different slant. The two dreams interlaced to form a fascinating mosaic.

Here is Pam's account:

Jim and I lay down, side by side, in a wooden box-like shape which opened at the top. We held hands and began a meditation based on the use of sexual energy. Within a few moments, our meditation deepened and our identities merged in a bodiless state. After what seemed to be an infinite period of time, we each returned to our separate bodies. I awakened immediately, knowing that Jim had participated in the experience. I waited for him to wake up; then I asked him what he had dreamt.

My dream went as follows:

The dream matched Pam's exactly until the time our meditation began to expand. My awareness blanked out for awhile, and when I came back to the dream I asked Pam what had happened. She told me we had merged. Apparently, I couldn't bring back the memory of the episode. Perhaps the intensity of the higher consciousness proved too much for me. Just after Pam finished describing the experience of merging, I awakened, and Pam asked me to give her the details of what I had dreamt.

Mutual dreams can easily go unrecognized. Except in special cases, there seems to be little way of identifying a mutual dream as such until after the fact. However, as the class demonstrated, it is possible to create a situation which favors sharing dreams. To take this experimentation a step further, the dreamer needs to be aware of dreaming while the dream takes place.

Pam and I also shared the following dream. Since I was lucid in the dream, I was able to experiment with the mutual dream terrain. This dream is taken from my book, *Dream Reality*:

(My account) I had just walked down the mountain in the dream when I met Pam outside a small house. We

walked inside and sat down on the wooden floor beside some other people. I knew I was dreaming and could tell by an increasing feeling of tiredness that I was about to wake up. Since I wanted to do something with my lucidity before being forced awake, I asked the group to observe me as I left the dream state consciously. Then I woke myself up.

(Pam's account) My memory of the dream begins with me waiting for Jim at the foot of a mountain. Then the scene shifts and I am sitting on the floor of a house with a group of people. One of the persons in the group began to fade out, and as he did so he told us to observe him, since he was tired and was going to leave the dream state. His image became darker and darker. Finally, there was just a hole where his body used to be. I thought of the black holes in space and the theory that they were portals to another dimension. I knew he had gone through to the waking state. Then I woke up.[20]

An interesting facet of this set of dreams is that I could tell by an increasing feeling of *tiredness* that I was about to awaken. Naturally, I had to fall asleep to get into the dream in the first place. But I experienced leaving the dream by means of the same process. This imputes an equal validity to both waking and dream states, implying that "falling asleep" is a metaphor for transition in consciousness. Ideas of this sort present a picture of the nature of dreaming quite different from the traditional psychological model. Dreams in general, not just mutual ones, may not depend upon waking state sensory stimuli as much as is commonly supposed.

Of course, how you respond to the whole question of the reality of dreams depends upon your perspective. From within the dream, waking state events often take a subsidiary role. The situation reverses itself when you are

[20]Donahoe, p. 52.

"awake."

Another prominent feature of the above "black hole" dream is its theme of reversal. My image turns into a shadow, a negative image. The "black hole," with its science fiction role as doorway to an anti-matter universe, further implies reversal.

These ideas of reversal and journey play a kind of "through the looking glass" theme. But perhaps the most interesting part is that I myself became the "hole" which led to the waking state. The movement between dream and waking states represents a transformation of consciousness, not a literal journey from one "space" to another.

Experimenters can study mutual dreams as altered states of consciousness, as dreams and as paranormal events. Spontaneous cases may occur too infrequently for detailed study. But the fact that mutual dreams can be encouraged experimentally helps potential explorers a great deal.

The mere existence of mutual dreams shows that dreaming is more complex than previously supposed. Statements normally made about dreams as a whole may be true for some kinds and not for others. Examining various dream types, including mutual dreams, will help to point beyond the limits of "ordinary" dream experiences and approaches.

Cultural Consensus and Mutual Dreams

The "primacy" of waking state events is a matter of consensus. Events which are just as perceptually vivid and "real," such as certain dream and visionary experiences, are not usually considered as valid as waking state events. Experiences of the former type are labelled "symbolic," "hallucinatory" or "subjective," meaning that they have some kind of validity, but one subordinate to, and dependent upon, the waking state. For mutual dreams, certainly, this devaluation will not hold.

Mutual dreams are as consensually verifiable and perceptually vivid as waking state events. However, they take place in an environment other than what is considered to be the normal one. People in the midst of a mutual dream, if observed by others in the waking state, would seem to be lying still with eyes closed. In normal circumstances, the mutual dreamers and their waking state observers would be aware of different perceptual environments. It begs the question to say that a mutual dream or a mutual OOB is just a mutual hallucination, as if the term "mutual hallucination" explains the phenomena away. The consensual verifiability of such events points to the conclusion that an order of experience is involved which is just as valid as waking state, physical phenomena.

Mutual dreams raise questions which require answers from intuitive sources and from experienced explorers. Among these questions are: Does out-of-body experience indicate that your identity is capable of surviving physical death? What is the relationship of these alternate "environments" to the waking state? And, what are the implications of such experiences for our understanding of the nature of the waking state?

The popular literature of the occult tradition supplies insufficient answers to such questions. The elaborate cosmologies found in many of these writings are not grounded solidly enough in actual exploration to be satisfying. Many occultist assertions are not really explanations, but rather imaginative devices which can enable readers to expand their experience.

Nevertheless, researchers have come up with answers (sometimes tentative ones) to some major questions. Those people who explore out-of-body experience or mutual dreaming, for example, generally come away convinced that the "primacy" of waking state experience is mainly a matter of cultural convention. An insistence upon the primacy of the waking state may be initially helpful for physical survival, but once survival needs are met, such insistence need not be maintained so rigidly.

As Pearce,[21] Lilly[22] and others suggest, the end of psychological dependence upon the belief in the primacy of waking state phenomena means the end of the fear of death. Concern for, and anxiety about, survival may well be the initial stages of a human growth process which eventually transcends such concerns. As these writers point out, survival anxiety inhibits the development of creativity, particularly the kind of creativity exhibited by mutual dreams, OOB's and similar kinds of experience.

The exploration of mutual dreams makes possible the ability to look at the universe as a continuum of possible plot lines, among which the waking state is only one. However, if you consider mutual dreams and the paranormal in a larger context, the ramifications are greater. The implication of such phenomena, then, is not centered upon the presentation of a new world-view of multiple environments. Nor do the major potentials of paranormal abilities lie in their capacity to transform waking state phenomena by yet to be discovered laws. The most important implication is that the paranormal may represent the boundary-surpassing capability of the human mind—the ability to create events, and if necessary, to invent laws to "justify" the existence of such events.

This idea precludes the assumption, often held in occultism, that there exists a multitude of worlds ("planes," etc.) which can be visited just as different countries can be visited on Earth. If the psyche "precedes" space-time, then there can be no "geography of the mind."

Of course, to propose that mutual dreams and the paranormal are part of the human ability to suspend consen-

[21] Joseph Chilton Pearce, *The Crack in the Cosmic Egg* (New York: Pocket Books, 1971), pp. 167-168.

[22] John C. Lilly, *The Center of the Cyclone* (New York: Bantam, 1972), p. 33, p. 81.

sual agreements about what can and cannot happen in the world raises new questions. One of these is: Beyond philosophical speculation, what can be done with these conclusions? In theory it may be possible to do anything; whether you can or cannot do any particular feat is a matter for experiential discovery.

In a way, the situation people encounter here in the waking state is like that encountered in a lucid dream: some things can be changed around by conscious intent alone, and easily, while others cannot. The absence of paranormal powers is as much a puzzle as the presence of them. The enigma requires that researchers both develop new theories and personally explore the mysteries in view.

4

At Play in the Beyond: Swedenborg, Van Eeden and the World of Dreams

Parallels in Trance and Dream

Emanuel Swedenborg, Swedish scientist and inner explorer (1688-1772), began his psychological experimentation at the age of 56, after nearly exhausting a large number of the available natural sciences. His research led him directly into what he believed to be contacts with the dead, and with mystical experiences beyond. Some rather convincing accounts of his paranormal abilities exist, generally consisting of information obtained from the "spirits." One particularly interesting example of this concerns John Wesley, the founder of Methodism. In February 1772, Wesley received a letter from Swedenborg, which the former read aloud to other preachers present. In the letter, Swedenborg informed Wesley that a meeting between the two of them would be fine—and that Swedenborg had been told "in the world of spirits" that Wesley desired to visit. Wesley told onlookers that he in fact had wanted to meet Swedenborg, but had not mentioned it to anyone. No doubt impressed, Wesley wrote back saying that he was leaving for a journey of six months, but that he would visit upon his return.

Swedenborg politely replied that, to his regret, this visit would not come to pass since he would be dying on the 29th day of the following month. Swedenborg, to all appearances healthy, did die on that date—a date which he gave to others weeks in advance as well.

Though Swedenborg lived a long life, had fore-knowledge of his own death (and apparently the deaths of others on occasion), investigated breath control and in other ways lived like some advanced yogic practitioners, he did have his differences. He avoided alcohol and ate sparingly, but, for the last 14 years of his life, the vast bulk of his diet consisted of sweet cakes, coffee and milk with lots of sugar added, and an occasional roll boiled in milk. He indulged in snuff so greatly that what spilled between the pages of his writing helped preserve his manuscripts from insects. While at home, Swedenborg felt freed of the obligation of observing somewhat normal waking hours. There he went into his inner explorations whenever the mood occurred. Sometimes that mood lasted for days at a time. He worked alone, totally without fixed schedules of sleep and waking time. Nevertheless, this inner exploration coupled with his prodigious writing efforts did not prevent him from meeting and speaking with friends and otherwise acting like a normal (circa the 1770's in Sweden) human being.

Swedenborg conducted his spiritual journeys through the use of trance.[1] He followed the procedure common to

---

[1] In this chapter and the following one, I am using "trance" to designate the act of complete mental absorption, usually accompanied by deep physical relaxation.

Theodore Barber and his associates have advanced a convincing case for the idea that the "hypnotic state" or "trance state" is a misnomer. They contend that the subject's expectations, both those developed from past exposure to the concept of hypnosis, and those given by the "hypnotist," help shape the experiential characteristics of the subject's "trance." Barber now prefers to use the phrase "creative all those who investigate trance, whether that investigation is defined clinically (as in hypnosis research) or spiritually (as in meditative practices). The procedure simply consists of entering a deep state of relaxation with a high degree of alertness. What happens next depends upon a number of things, including the explorer's expectations and beliefs about what can happen. Contrary to popular misconception, trance, including ''hypnotic'' trance does not require that the subject (1) lose alertness, (2) surrender his or her will to that of the hypnotist, or (3) forget the experience immediately after it (amnesia). The work of Theodore Barber and his colleagues (see bibliography), my own studies of the area, and Charles Tart's experiment in mutual hypnosis (discussed later in this chapter) all indicate that subjects *may* choose to retain their full volitional capacities during trance, even if their entry into the process is initiated by someone else.

The extreme fluidity of possibilities in trance experience makes it very difficult to judge the validity of trance events. In fact, as I have explained elsewhere,[2] it no longer makes sense to ask if any altered state experience is valid. Any experience is ''valid,'' the question is what kind of experience is it? For example, was the event consensually verifiable; i.e., did more than one person remember taking part? What was the perceptual quality

---

imagination'' in place of hypnosis, and when he does use the latter word, he places it within quotation marks. See the bibliography section, ''Psychological Perspectives,'' for references.

I use the word ''trance'' here to accommodate readers who are not familiar with the nonstate approach and writers, like Swedenborg and Van Eeden, who use the word frequently. For me to substitute another phrase could create confusion.

[2]James J. Donahoe, *Dream Reality* (Oakland, CA: Bench Press, rev. ed., 1979), pp. 115-116.

of the experience? The same questions and concerns apply to the study of dreams.

If all trance and dream experiences were purely personal affairs, subsidiary to, and dependent upon, waking sense perception, then their exploration would be of very limited significance. Orthodox opinion in the intellectual community has held that these experiences are purely personal, but research in paranormal, dream and altered state experience contradicts this conception. A psychotherapeutic approach to dreams and other altered states of consciousness (ASC's) does nothing to challenge the orthodox view. Neither does the use of lucid dreaming for such purposes as problem-solving, psychological insight and aesthetic inspiration.

Two major lines of inquiry will radically alter the traditional, though antiquated, understanding of the nature of trance experience, once researchers grasp their significance. Charles Tart followed one of these lines in an experiment he conducted on mutual hypnosis.[3] In the experiment, Tart helped two subjects to enter an apparently mutual trance environment and to return with full memory of their adventures. The subjects seem to have experienced the trance environment at least as vividly as they experience the waking state counterpart. An additional interesting feature of this experiment is that the subjects chose to sever ties with Tart, who intended to retain the status of hypnotist-control. They used his help as a springboard to domains which drew their attention.

The second line of inquiry regarding trance reveals that subjects can use trance to perceive events paranormally. This paranormal perception may take the form of out-of-body experience, telepathy, or some other mode. Research on trance-related paranormal perception occupies

[3]Charles Tart, "Psychedelic Experiences Associated with a Novel Hypnotic Procedure, Mutual Hypnosis," *Altered States of Consciousness*, ed. Charles Tart (Garden City, NY: Anchor, 1972), pp. 297-315.

much of the history of formal parapsychological study, including the studies of both the English and the American Society for Psychical Research.

These two discoveries, that a trance experience may be consensually verifiable, and that it may contain paranormal information, imply that researchers must accord at least some ASC experiences with as much validity as they do the waking state. What holds for trance experience applies equally well, in this case, to dreams. In the earlier chapter on mutual dreams, I present parallels in dreaming to what Tart illustrated with hypnosis.[4] Paranormal perception is, if anything, more common in dreams than in trance. And yet dream events, like trance experiences, have been considered somehow "less real" and less important than waking state events.

All this is prologue to saying that an experience can no longer be dismissed by calling it "just a dream" or "self-hypnosis." Swedenborg investigated trance; Van Eeden, a 20th century Dutch physicist, experimented with lucid dreaming. For researchers to adequately appreciate the efforts of Swedenborg and Van Eeden, the work of these two must be considered in a larger context than that of "purely personal" inner exploration.

There are significant similarities in the discoveries of Swedenborg and Van Eeden, though the two authors worked within different frameworks. Swedenborg wrote from a strongly theological orientation; the great majority of his volumes are concerned with the symbolism of the Bible, although his personal experimental records pertain to the kind of research that explorers today find helpful.

[4]Spontaneous, mutual "trance" experiences have been reported throughout the history of psychical research. Shared "hallucinations," collectively perceived apparitions and similar phenomena are described in the full article by Hornell and Ella B. Hart listed in the bibliography. The idea that mutual "trance" experience occurs, does not depend upon the Tart experiment alone.

During his time, those who explored the powers of the creative imagination, including its paranormal dimensions, usually classified their work under the general category of religion. Psychology did not exist as a separate discipline, and few explorers had the ability of William Blake to translate their studies into the vocabulary of art.

Van Eeden, who wrote 150 years after Swedenborg, faced a different situation. Afraid that his experiences were too controversial for a wide public, he chose to convey them through fiction, in particular his novel, *The Bride of Dreams.*[5]

In *The Bride of Dreams,* the narrator's experiments with lucid dreams lead him into an ongoing sleep-state encounter with a previous lover. This accentuates difficulties he has with his waking state wife. Later on, he meets another woman in his dreams, who eventually becomes his second *waking state* wife. The narrator speaks directly to the reader through all of this, but not all of the book is taken up with domestic entanglements. Instead, Van Eeden, through the voice of the narrator, lectures on matters of religious conviction and on the possibilities of dream exploration.

Van Eeden himself explains his use of the fictional format in a paper for the Society for Psychical Research:

> . . . The fictitious form enabled me to deal freely with delicate matters, and had also the advantage that it expressed rather unusual ideas in a less aggressive way—esoterically, so to speak. Yet I want to express these ideas also in a form that will appeal more directly to the scientific mind, and I know I cannot find a better audience for this purpose than the members of the Society for Psychical Research, who are accustomed to treat investigations and

<hr>

[5]Frederik Van Eeden, *The Bride of Dreams*, tr. Mellie Von Auw (New York: Mitchell Kennerly, 1913).

ideas of an unusual sort in a broad-minded and yet critical spirit.[6]

Fortunately, the paper Van Eeden submitted to the Society for Psychical Research (SPR) contains enough factual material on his dream journeys for readers to extrapolate correctly from the author's fiction, since the parallels are clear.

Though both Swedenborg and Van Eeden used a different procedure for their investigations, both explored the same domain. Today, consciousness researchers realize that one method, such as trance or dreaming, can lead into many kinds of experience. Distinctions between trance, meditation, and dreaming are drawn by researchers primarily for the sake of convenience. Though the three activities represent different verbal categories, they do not reflect distinctly different modes of consciousness.

There are many striking similarities in the realms mapped by Swedenborg and Van Eeden—similarities which reinforce the notion that trance and dreaming are not so dissimilar after all. Both explorers felt, at times, that they were in contact with the dead. In Swedenborg's case this supposition was backed by correct paranormal information apparently retrieved from "spirits" he met.[7] In one case, Swedenborg seems to have communicated with the "spirit" of a dead man who then told Swedenborg the location of a receipt, thus proving that a debt claimed against the dead man's wife was false. Swedenborg's information gave exact details on the location of the receipt; it was found placed in a hidden drawer, known only to the dead man—the place Swedenborg described. It seems that Swedenborg contacted "spirits" for mundane,

[6]Frederik Van Eeden, "A Study of Dreams," *Altered States of Consciousness*, p. 147.

[7]George Trobridge, *Swedenborg: Life and Teaching* (New York: Swedenborg Foundation, 1962), pp. 194-209.

though worthy, causes such as the preceding one only when asked. Sometimes a person would ask for an exchange of messages with a recently deceased relative or friend and Swedenborg would oblige, to show the questioner evidence for the survival of death. One person who reportedly asked Swedenborg for this assistance was the Queen of Sweden, and, so goes the story, she was overcome by Swedenborg's reply. In reference to what the visionary told her, she said, "Only God knows this."

In addition to visiting the dead, both Swedenborg and Van Eeden reported travels in a "second body" which had the ability to sense just as completely and intensely as the physical body. They described entering spheres of exalted beauty where sensation became revelatory and ecstatic. They also discussed areas where unpleasant beings resided. Swedenborg called these beings "infernal spirits" and their place of residence "hell." Van Eeden's term for them was "demons."

Their writings show that both authors believed that their explorations revealed something of importance regarding life after death. Both felt they had experienced the after-death state while still living. OOB experimenters today often reach the same conclusion about their own out-of-body experience. The similarity among reports of those describing death-bed experiences, people who have come close to death and then been resuscitated, OOB experimenters and psychedelic voyagers, helps support the idea that the after-death state may be explored by the living.[8]

Van Eeden writes confidently of his conclusions about the after-death state with the following words:

[8]For examples of what those who are brought back from the verge of death experience, as well as the experiences of those who complete the transition, see: Karlis Osis and Erlendur Haraldsson, *At the Hour of Death* (New York: Avon, 1977).

The insensible world is not full of pure loftiness and unmixed nobility. I do not constantly wander there in Elysian fields, absorbed in flowing conversations regarding important questions with spectres of noble stature and dignified bearing. As all reality, the reality of the beyond is unexpectedly fantastic, full of surprises and full of disillusions; but on the whole more stimulating and more beautiful than anything the imagination has pictured regarding it. And this is of supreme importance in the practice of our daily life—that the insensible world is in part our own creation, subject to our will, built up from the conclusions gathered in our day-life, with the faculties and powers which by practice and use we have in this same life made our own. To say for this reason that nothing new awaits us would be equal to the assertion that Beethoven had given nothing new to the world, because, after all, he only employed combinations of familiar sounds and tones. I again repeat—nothing in our actual day-life can equal the ecstasy of even a single awakening in the new sphere.[9]

As Van Eeden continues, he anticipates the arguments of those who will call his journeys mere flights of the imagination:

Does it make much difference whether we give to one and the same thing, vehemently and intensely felt, the name of fancy or the name of reality?—and does anyone know a reliable mark of distinction between the two? Everything is the product of imagination. . . .[10]

Exploring the After-Death Terrain

Swedenborg used the hypnagogic and hypnopompic states as gateways for much of his exploration. The hypnagogic state is the transition point between waking and

[9]Van Eeden, *The Bride of Dreams*, p. 228.
[10]Van Eeden, p. 229.

sleeping, as you are falling asleep. As you begin to awaken, you pass through the hypnopompic state. Each state represents a transition between waking and sleeping; the difference between each state lies in whether it occurs at the beginning (hypnagogic) or end (hypnopompic) of the sleep cycle. Either time can be helpful for inner exploration, although Swedenborg felt that the hypnopompic stage brought with it an unequalled peacefulness and clarity. He writes of the sense of vision accessible during the hypnopompic stage in the following passage:

> . . . Another vision is that between the time of sleep and the time of wakefulness, when the man is waking up, and has not yet shaken off sleep from his eyes. This is the sweetest of all, for heaven then operates into his rational mind in the utmost tranquility.[11]

The kind of consistent attention Swedenborg brought to bear upon the hypnagogic and hypnopompic stages made his sleep a testing ground for many varieties of visionary activity. Swedenborg's term for this kind of revelatory experience was "preternatural sleep." Since he did not have the vocabulary now available to differentiate among various states of consciousness, Swedenborg recorded all his night-time dreams, visions and ecstasies in his *Journal of Dreams*.[12] Eventually, he gained access to visionary faculties in the waking state as well, sometimes without the need for any special procedure to induce these experiences.

Wilson Van Dusen, a contemporary commentator, illuminates Swedenborg's conception of trance with the following observations:

[11]Quoted in: Wilson Van Dusen, *The Presence of Other Worlds* (New York: Perennial Library, 1974), p. 28.

[12]Emanuel Swedenborg, *The Journal of Dreams*, tr. James John Garth Wilkinson, *Studia Swedenborgiana*, Nos. 1-4, Vol. I (Newton, MA: Swedenborg School of Religion, 1974-1975).

. . . In the trance inner experiences are no longer delicate and faint, but are clear, intense, and real. Personal awareness still exists, but bodily awareness is less or lost altogether. . . . there is a feeling of intensified consciousness but a paralysis of the body.[13]

Swedenborg also experimented with a king of yogic meditative procedure. He focused upon a problem or question with intense concentration, allowing his breathing to become so faint that it seemed to cease completely.[14] Like many practitioners of yoga, Swedenborg discovered a correlation between breath and thought. He observed differences in the rhythm of his breathing and charted the corresponding changes in consciousness that accompanied such variations. He found that in intense ecstasy, breath ceased together with thought. In his *Journal of Dreams,* Swedenborg records:

. . . in ecstasy or trance the man holds his breath; at this time the thoughts are, in a manner of speaking, away. Likewise in sleep, when both inspiration and expiration belong to nature; when that is represented which flows in from a higher source.[15]

Swedenborg regarded his dreams as symbolic commentaries upon his behavior in the waking state. He explored hypnagogic, hypnopompic and trance experience with great interest and perseverance, though the possibilities of lucid dreaming apparently never crossed his mind. Van Eeden, in contrast, made lucid dreaming his main form of inner exploration. He too had a number of experiences during sleep which are perhaps better classed as visionary or out-of-body experiences. It is important to remember, however, that these categories blend into one another. For example, Van Eeden spoke of a ''dream body'' in exactly the same way as an OOB experimenter might refer to the

[13]Van Dusen, p. 19

[14]Van Dusen, p. 19.

[15]Swedenborg, *The Journal of Dreams*, No. 2, p. 20.

"second body." Van Eeden's classification of "initial dreams" seems very close to what Van Dusen defines as trance. The following is part of Van Eeden's description of "initial dreams":

> . . . It occurs only in the very beginning of sleep . . . . In hypnagogic hallucinations we have visions, but we have full bodily perception. In the initial dream type I see and feel as in any other dream. . . . all perceptions of the physical body . . . are entirely absent.[16]

Reports of dream and trance explorations raise an important question—how can you determine, when lucid in a trance or dream, that someone you encounter is not a purely personal hallucination? In Swedenborg's case, the issue revolved around the "spirits" he met. He spent long hours wondering whether they were really fantasies instead of what they appeared to be. The verified paranormal information he returned with in some cases provides at least partial corroboration for his belief that his contacts with the "spirits" were genuine, at least partially.

For Van Eeden, this question about the status of people encountered "outside" the waking state concerned the figures he met in lucid dreams. Students of mutual dreams often encounter the same problem. When you have experienced several verified mutual dreams, you become tempted to regard every dream figure you meet, at least those in lucid dreams, as more than a simple product of your imagination. With most mutual dreams, at least you have the chance of checking out the content by talking to people who appeared in your dream. The issue becomes more complex when you have lucid dream encounters with

[16]Van Eeden, "A Study of Dreams," *Altered States of Consciousness*, p. 148.

someone who is dead. In one encounter of this kind, Van Eeden chose the reasonable course of asking the dream figure for an opinion. In this particular dream he met Prof. van't Hoff, a famous Dutch chemist whom Van Eeden had known. According to Van Eeden:

> I asked first why we, lacking our organs of sense, could arrive at any certainty that the person to whom we were talking was really that person and not a subjective illusion. Then van't Hoff said: "Just as in common life; by a general impression."
>
> "Yet," I said, "in common life there is stability of observation and there is consolidation by repeated observation."
>
> "Here also," said van't Hoff. "And the sensation of *certainty* is the same."[17]

The similarities among the experiences of Swedenborg, Van Eeden, OOB experimenters, people who have undergone near-death episodes and other ASC explorers indicate that ASC's may be excellent vehicles for studying the after-death state while alive. To try to map the after-death state is as difficult as to attempt to chart the out-of-body "terrain"; the territory changes to accommodate the observer. What is being observed does not have the relatively fixed quality of waking state geography. Swedenborg seems to have known this on some occasions and forgotten it on others. On one hand, he writes that "heaven and hell" (the after-death states) are reflections of the residents' inner states. On the other hand, he describes heaven in geographical terms, explaining the different types of population and habitations to be found, depending upon whether you visit the northern, southern, eastern or western regions.[18]

[17]Van Eeden, p. 156.

[18]Emanuel Swedenborg, *Heaven and Hell* (New York: Swedenborg Foundation, 1974), pp. 84-90.

Swedenborg's depiction of the after-life is interesting and valuable, but its provinciality provides a good lesson for others interested in the same subject. For example, in discussing the instruction given to those who have died, he writes:

> . . . the Mohammedans receive instruction from angels who had been previously in the same religion and had been converted to Christianity . . . .
> . . . the Mohammedans and heathen, are taught from doctrines suited to their apprehension, which differ from heavenly doctrine only in this, that spiritual life is taught by means of moral life in harmony with the good tenets of their religion . . .[19]

Swedenborg does not seem to have realized that he also could be receiving instruction in "doctrines suited to his apprehension."

Hopefully, contemporary explorers of the same realm will try to avoid making Swedenborg's mistakes. The assumption that a simple, dualistic logic is sufficient for dealing with inner experience leads into the very kinds of difficulties that Swedenborg encountered. Since he felt his revelations were either fact or fantasy, he left himself little room in between.

One of the major discoveries for which both Swedenborg and Van Eeden deserve credit is the importance of normal, waking state life in regard to the ASC's they investigated. Anticipating Jung's concept of synchronicity, Swedenborg advanced a theory of correspondences in which inner and outer events are seen to reflect each other. Swedenborg felt that "man after death continues to eternity such as his will, or ruling love is."[20] Since in his view, the core of any person was that person's deepest

---

[19]Swedenborg, p. 365.
[20]Swedenborg, p. 330.

inclinations and desires, he believed that people developed the same quality of self-expression in death that they had in life.

In this extract from a quote given earlier, Van Eeden voices a closely related idea:

> . . .And this is of supreme importance in the practice of our daily life—that the insensible world is in part our own creation, subject to our will, built up from the conclusions gathered in our day-life, with the faculties and powers which by practice and use we have in this same life made our own.[21]

What you do with your awareness during the day affects your dreams. The reverse is also true: your dream actions can exert a powerful effect upon your waking state. Events in either state are valid. Conscious intent developed in one carries through into the other. The principles for structuring experience are the same for all states: conscious intent and the powers of imagination.

[21]Van Eeden, *The Bride of Dreams*, p. 228.

Part II:

Paradigmatic

Frontiers

5

Hypnosis Reformulated:
Psychology and
the Creative Imagination

The work of experimenters in recent years supports the idea that ''hypnosis'' does not exist in the form of a specific, discrete state of consciousness.[1] Dr. Theodore X. Barber and his colleagues argue convincingly that the ''hypnotic'' or ''trance'' state is a misnomer for an intensified responsiveness on the part of the subject. Researchers in the field discovered long ago that a subject's depth of ''trance'' and the effectiveness of suggestion are two separate variables. The ''nonstate'' theorists go further and point out that what a subject experiences as ''trance'' depends upon that person's expectations.

Dr. Barber agrees that ''hypnotic'' phenomena can be induced and utilized in intriguing ways, but he disagrees with the old ''trance paradigm'' which purports to explain how these phenomena occur. He prefers to use the phrase

---

[1]For references to this experimentation consult the article (listed in the bibliography) by Theodore Barber entitled ''Suggested ('hypnotic') Behavior: The Trance Paradigm Vs. an Alternative Paradigm.'' This 66-page paper includes 10 pages of bibliography.

''creative imagination'' in place of ''hypnosis,'' and he places the latter word within quotation marks to indicate the fallacious (in his view) connotations of the word. Commonly produced ''hypnotic'' tasks include control of psychosomatic symptoms, memory enhancement, self-induced anesthesia and selective alteration of sensory perceptions.

A major insight afforded by Dr. Barber's view is that the trance induction techniques, deemed essential by hypnotists for so long, are unnecessary. Even more important, the nonstate approach provides a context which is non-authoritarian (the subject retains control), non-amnesic (full memory is retained when the subject so desires), and highly alert (in contrast to the drowsiness formerly associated with ''hypnotic'' process). It is clear that Dr. Barber's use of the phrase ''creative imagination,'' as a substitute for ''hypnosis,'' is very similar in meaning to my own term, ''conscious intent.''

As I point out here and in *Dream Reality,* the faculty of conscious intent has possibilities far beyond the phenomena traditionally associated with ''hypnosis.'' Parapsychological phenomena, altered states of consciousness and special dream types can all be clarified by using ''conscious intent'' or ''creative imagination'' to label the core process involved.

We can better understand the importance of these changes in the terminology and practice of ''hypnosis'' by viewing the historical origins of the method.

Historical Boundaries
and Imaginative Realities

Although James Braid coined the term ''hypnotism'' in the 1840's, credit for discovery of the phenomenon is usually given to Franz Anton Mesmer, whose demonstrations of ''animal magnetism'' (later called mesmerism) astounded Paris in the 1770's and 1780's. Mesmer believed in a material interpretation of the phenomenon he investigated. His idea of a "magnetic fluid" which emanated from the magnetizer to the patient, and which could be enhanced when the magnetizer kept magnets on his person, met with disfavor from the medical orthodoxy of his day. They directed their criticisms at his explanation, not at the validity of the effects he claimed to produce. The Commissioners from the Faculty of Medicine, who investigated and promptly denounced Mesmer, behaved as if unusual facts could not be valid without an acceptable theory being present to explain them.

The traditional medical techniques of Mesmer's time, such as bloodletting and the use of emetics, probably did more to kill the patient than cure him. Thus, Mesmer suffered an irony compounded; his treatment worked as well or better than the accepted ones, but he misunderstood its method of operation. And that misunderstanding, the material "explanation" of magnetic healing, seemed to be the only kind of explanation the medical community could agree to consider.

Rejection by the scientific orthodoxy of the period probably encouraged magnetizers in their search for more exotic terrains. By this time Mesmer had asserted that *all* illness came from disturbances in the body's natural magnetic fluid; a position which could only heighten opposition from official medicine. (Strangely enough, a variant of this theory gained public attention again recently, in the Chinese formulation of *ch'i,* used as the basis for acupuncture practice.) Soon magnetizers conducted sessions for magical information about the past, communication with the deceased, telepathy, precognition, and revelations about the after-life.

As the magnetizers turned their attention to more and more unusual phenomena, their practices gained wide popularity among the common people, while losing ground in medical circles. To revive the use of "magnetic sleep" in medicine, James Braid suggested the word "neuro-hypnotism," which he eventually shortened to "hypnotism." He derived the word from the Greek *hypnos,* meaning sleep. Other English physicians, notably the surgeons Elliotson and Esdaile, reported the usefulness of "magnetic sleep" in anesthesia. However, the discovery of general anesthetics soon stopped this temporary resurgence of medical interest.

Public enthusiasm for "animal magnetism," and its descendants, helped to promote spiritualism and to encourage the birth of various metaphysical and occult movements. The popularization of the benefits of suggestion still goes on today in the form of systems which advocate positive thought and visualization as a counter to life's problems. Mediumship, "hypnotic" regression to "previous incarnations," attempts to stimulate artistic and musical creativity by means of suggestion, and the inner search for revelatory information about the physical world were all explored avidly by experimenters in the 1800's; the same quests continue.

During the 19th century, explorers consulted Ouija boards, wrote trance-inspired volumes and studied cases of multiple personality. For scientists, the reputable applications of "hypnosis" became its psychiatric ones. Meanwhile, spiritualistic practitioners considered "trance" as a valid means of communicating with great figures of the past and as a key to expanding paranormal powers. As the gulf between the scientific and metaphysical communities widened, official science restricted its scope of inquiry. "Unofficial" explorations extended as far as the explorers' imaginations would permit. These same explorers often suffered from the credulity which sc frequently accompanies cultic approaches to altered states and the paranormal.

Some participants on the "unofficial" side accepted quite literally a great deal of garbled and naive information obtained through the use of "trance." Information of this sort included the usual assemblage of strange "facts" regarding life on other planets, the ancient history of the Earth and the nature of the after-death state.

By the early 1900's, "trance" exploration yielded literary productions as well, among them the novels and poems of Pearl Lenore Curran, dictated by a "trance personality" named Patience Worth.[2] Curran's novels, written in old English dialects, contained historical information which puzzled researchers who tried to check the authenticity of Patience Worth. Worth claimed to have lived in 17th century England.

The above brief outline of some of the history of "hypnosis" illustrates the reluctance of the scientific orthodoxy, then as today, to admit the physiological influence of psychological processes. Even where this influence is acknowledged, sharp limitations are presumed. The two avenues through which "hypnosis" gained limited acceptance within the scientific mainstream, medicine and psychotherapy, implicitly limit the applications of the process. This is natural, as practitioners of healing will apply their tools to their own art and discard discoveries which lead in other directions.

Put simply, the traditional ideas about "hypnosis" exist because they do the least to trouble established belief in the archaic doctrines of mechanistic determinism, and in the presumed limitations of the powers of the human mind. Taken a few steps further, the "creative imagination" proposed by Barber and his colleagues can include parapsychological acts, such as self-induced telepathy and precognition, as easily as self-induced anesthesia. As scientists are realizing, there is nothing inherently unscientific about applying familiar tools to unfamiliar domains. To attempt to self-induce out-of-body experience is as valid as to attempt intentional relaxation. The same empiricism can apply to both, and most important, the same autonomy on the part of the experimenter-subject.

"Hypnosis" redefined opens the way for new explora-

---

[2]Henri F. Ellenberger, *The Discovery of the Unconscious* (New York: Basic Books, 1970), pp. 163-164.

tions of human volition, conducted by the subject, not upon the subject. Dr. Barber notes the need for this non-authoritarian approach. Other writers, such as Colin Wilson, show how much this transition means in regard to the evolution of the scientific, philosophical and psychological thought of recent centuries. Arthur Koestler has described in detail some of the major implications of the current paradigm shift, in physics as well as parapsychology. Two sets of boundaries vanish at once; the first, consisting of ''laws'' as to what events can possibly occur, and the second, consisting of ''laws'' regarding what an individual mind can and cannot accomplish. The recognition that human beings can do the remarkable things recorded in the annals of ''hypnosis'' and parapsychology bears striking resemblance to the Renaissance conception of ''imagination,'' an idea which stretched far beyond the simple, aesthetic notion commonly held in following centuries, including our own. It is no accident that our historical appraisal of the Renaissance is undergoing the radical transformations sustained by other disciplines. The works of Frances Yates stand as major contributions to this particular endeavor.

To extend the application of ''creative imagination,'' or ''conscious intent,'' beyond mainstream ''hypnotic'' phenomena to parapsychological acts, and no further, would be unnecessarily limiting. Interesting results in the volitional use of dreams, including lucid, high and mutual dream types, indicate that special dream types should be included in this realm of exploration.

Transpersonal psychology consists of the study of human possibilities which transcend the norm. These include parapsychological acts, special dream types, voluntary control of physiological processes and altered states of consciousness. The reformulation of ''hypnosis'' allows for two key emphases: the volitional exploration of such areas by subjects and the use of directed imagination to facilitate such exploration. From this new vantage point, "suggestibility" becomes a potential talent.[3]

Mesmer's Mistake

Mesmer's methods worked; he misunderstood why. His mistake, the attempt to reduce psychologically-based phenomena to the terms of the natural sciences, is repeated by others who want the kind of cultural approbation accorded official scientists. As the historical examples of Wilhelm Reich and "orgone energy," Karl von Reichenbach and "Odic force," and Mesmer and "animal magnetism" indicate, discoverers of "new" mental phenomena court danger when they seize physical explanations for their observations. Such action, contrary to the hopes of the discoverers, does not result in mass acceptance of the phenomena, nor does it encourage officially-sanctioned research. Once those in the natural sciences discredit the explanation, they ignore the phenomena as well. Rather than propose inadequate "scientific" theories to unify the great variety of ASC and paranormal experience under one roof, it may be more important simply to gather evidence and raise questions.

The field of psychology continues to labor under the ideological and political difficulties which faced Mesmer, and practitioners have worked out an uneasy compromise in which, ironically, Mesmer's mistaken theoretical approach has become the norm. Thomas Szasz, a psychiatrist and psychoanalyst, makes the following remarks:

[3]Dr. Sheryl Wilson and Dr. Barber have devised a new "suggestibility" scale in accord with the non-authoritarian strategies required by the new paradigm. The scale makes it possible to assess a subject's talents concerning traditional "hypnotic" tasks such as relaxation, arm levitation and so on. See "The Creative Imagination Scale," listed in the bibliography.

Freud never tired of asserting two contradictory claims: one, that it was not necessary that a person have medical or psychiatric qualifications to practice psychoanalysis; the other, that neuroses (and perversions, psychoses, etc.) were diseases. I think the reason for this was quite simple: on the one hand, he wanted to acquire the prestige and protection of medicine for the religious cult he was creating, and over which he wanted to rule—from the Bergasse while alive, and from the grave when dead; on the other hand, he knew, and realized that others would know, that conversation is not a form of medical treatment.[4]

In this quotation, and at length in his numerous works, Szasz undermines the medical pretensions of psychotherapists, pretensions which he believes inevitably play a politically repressive role. Psychology's imitation of the natural sciences can only ''succeed'' at the cost of reducing human beings to truly appropriate topics of scientific observation—objects.

Over forty years before Szasz made the above comments, another psychoanalyst, Otto Rank, came to very similar conclusions. Secretary to Freud and a member of Freud's early inner circle, Rank broke with Freud for several reasons. One of these was Rank's strong individuality, which could not remain indefinitely submerged in the role of submissive disciple. There was another reason for this separation, equally strong, and that was Rank's deep respect for the irrational in human nature. Rank felt that psychology ''killed the soul'' by elevating rational understanding above all else. As far as he was concerned, intellectual understanding by itself could neither heal psychological injury nor advance creativity. He believed that a more fundamental reorientation to the psyche was required, one which even the artist could only approximate.

At the First International Congress on Mental Hygiene,

---

[4]Thomas Szasz, *The Second Sin* (Garden City, NY: Anchor, 1973), p. 92.

on May 8, 1930 in Washington, D.C., Rank delivered a ten-minute address which included devastating comments upon psychology and psychoanalysis. Rank had no need to be part of the fraternity anymore; he was subsequently condemned as an enemy by many in the psychoanalytic movement. However, some of the major ideas in his talk are not only considered valid psychology these days, but they are also at the core of the movement towards a more humanistic psychotherapy. His remarks included the following:

> . . . Because I have gone through all the phases of the development of scientific psychology and its practical applications within the last twenty-five years, my extensive experience and study both theoretical and therapeutic has led me to the conviction that the scientific approach to human behavior and personality problems is not only insufficient but leaves out the most essential part of it, namely, the human side, the characteristic of which is just that it can't be measured and checked and controlled.[5]

The theme of central importance to Rank and Szasz, that psychology differs fundamentally from the natural sciences, extends to the study of the paranormal. Parapsychology, particularly in the last twenty-five years, has followed the example of psychology by looking to "scientific" status as a means of acquiring prestige.

Remedies of the Imagination

Another approach to the "science" of consciousness is needed, one which bypasses the natural sciences and which unifies the study of the paranormal, the psychology of consciousness, and the study of imagination. At a later

[5]Quotation included in: Jessie Taft, *Otto Rank* (New York: Julian Press, 1958), p. 148.

point, perhaps all this will come together with the natural sciences as well. However, at the moment, the study of consciousness needs to be granted a position which is independent. The key to accomplishing this lies, I think, in an examination of conscious intent and the imaginative faculties.

Conscious intent involves a kind of effort best described by the phrase "allowing it (the event desired) to happen." The difference between conscious intent and the strenuous action many associate with volition, is illustrated well by brainwave biofeedback. When people first produce alpha waves with the help of biofeedback equipment, they may be told by an observer to "try harder." The effort to do so immediately blocks the alpha wave production. A relaxed, "passive" will, however, can once again allow the alpha waves to continue. This form of volition, conscious intent, succeeds in many instances where a strong exertion of will cannot, particularly when the goal is to direct physiological or psychological processes.

On occasion, people introduced to the concept of conscious intent fear that the development of this faculty will somehow rob their inner life of spontaneity, perhaps even thwart the "natural" growth of their personality. Such anxiety is unjustified, because the kind of self-control exercised in conscious intent can be a cooperative and harmonious one, quite distinct from self-manipulation. The fear of consciously directing hitherto "involuntary" processes arises simply out of an unfamiliarity with the act. The argument that such conscious direction is "unnatural" presumes the superiority of what is mere habit, and belies the fact that personality itself, as well as language and culture, are constructs. Why cannot the creations of humanity be regarded as part of "nature" as well? And why should the uncontrollable facets of life be assumed to be beneficent, when so often experience teaches the opposite? The denigration of human will leads to a paralysis in which a person's sense of meaning is diminished rather than enhanced. To elevate conscious intent leads to its axis: the powers of imagination.

Like the psyche, the faculty of imagination is not limited to the world of facts, the world of the past. Imagination extends beyond the merely aesthetic into the very structure of waking state experience. As Thomas Kuhn, Michael Polanyi, Joseph Pearce and others have pointed out, perception is a creative act. Imagination creates the world, including those events which force a revision of world-view. Through the agency of conscious intent, imagination can be used to transform waking state experience.

"Paranormal" events form part of what is simply the transcendent function of the human mind. The benefit of having categories such as telepathy, out-of-body experience and so on is that they enable people who have not experienced such things to do so. It would be a mistake to think that, by constructing these categories, parapsychologists are delineating the limits of the paranormal. The paranormal cannot have limits in any final sense, any more than can the imaginative powers.

Imagination allows people to transcend the "real," by entertaining a vision of alternative possibilities—the paranormal act represents an actualization of such a vision. Since the process of actualized vision is what creates the waking state in the first place, it should not be surprising that the same function can be used to make changes.

6

Out-of-Body Experience: A Guide for Experimenters

In an out-of-body experience, the perceiver observes the environment from a location outside that of his or her physical body. Two kinds of out-of-body experiences (or OOB's) can be delineated. In the first, the classical OOB, the perceiver's focus shifts discretely to a single location apart from the physical body. The perceiver may be able to observe his or her body from this new vantage point. Most of the literature which describes OOB's discusses this particular type. In the second kind of out-of-body, the perceiver expands beyond normal body limits without discretely shifting to a separate location.

Implications and Experiments

It would seem that experimentation with OOB's would help determine their implications, but in this case the normal protocol is reversed. To understand which experiments are likely to produce significant results (and to whom they will be significant) we need to know something about the paradoxical nature of the phenomenon. First, OOB's are not clear-cut. They overlap with lucid dreams, some are consensually verifiable (in that they overlap with the normal, waking state environment), others take place in environments that bear little resemblance to anything on normal earth, and still others combine verifiable with ''hallucinatory'' (or ''extramundane'') content. We know all this from the many reports of OOB's already present in the literature. Yet laboratory investigators remain intent upon proving the validity of OOB research. They hope to do this by establishing the phenomenon's ''objective''; i.e., consensually verifiable, basis. After establishing that OOB's are not mere ''hallucinations,'' researchers would presumably go to work digging up psychophysiological correlates of OOB experience, training people to have ''reliable'' OOB's—and all kinds of funding would be forthcoming to accredit this branch of study in the eyes of society.

Unfortunately, there are fundamental errors involved in such an approach. Perhaps the primary one is that experimenters are using the presumptions of an archaic world-view (the existence of an ''objective'' universe, separate from the observer) to study a phenomenon which violates those same presumptions. Like mutual dreams, OOB's present disquieting questions to adherents of the conservative theory of mind (that the mind is generated by, and secondary to, the brain), a theory which is integrally connected to the old idea of an ''objective,'' physical world. These connections have to do with the importance of alternative perceptions, environments, and finally, alternative values.

Everything would be simplified if OOB's were either totally veridical (i.e., mapped on perfectly to the waking state environment) or totally non-verifiable, whenever they occurred. But not only can they be one or the other, they can perversely combine elements of both. This puts OOB's, like mutual dreams, somewhere in the interface between psychology and parapsychology, between physics and poetry, or perhaps more precisely, between the technological and the artistic imagination.

The "importance" or "validity" of studying OOB's depends in great part upon where the researcher stands in relation to the idea of the primacy of the waking state. To those inextricably caught in the old world-view, the OOB will seem to be like any other parapsychological or altered awareness event—a mildly interesting and rather unimportant anomaly. As a general means of obtaining usable information about the waking state, no paranormal ability comes close to the efficiency of technological means. But as an initial introduction to a world-view beyond waking state chauvinism, OOB's serve very well. And this latter use outweighs the others by far.

Research Pathways

The literature on OOB's makes it clear that unless we take a Procrustean approach, such experiences cannot be made to fit the traditional experimental frameworks. This is true for parapsychological phenomena in general, and is one reason why the field of parapsychology retains its near-invisible status. If we take one look at the physics of the early 1880's and another at the parapsychology of that time (when the Society for Psychical Research began), and compare their rate of progress, we see that something is drastically wrong. This is particularly irritating given the great promise of parapsychological study. Alternative methodologies need to be employed, but not all of these have to be new ones.

A prominent method of obtaining information about OOB's which continues to be used by researchers consists of gathering reports, then categorizing and assessing them. Celia Green's book, *Out-of-the-Body Experiences*, provides a good recent example of this approach. Since OOB's seem to occur spontaneously more often than not, even for experienced practitioners, a body of reports spanning the experiences of many people can be extremely helpful. Very few people can successfully induce an

OOB at all times, at least as far as researchers are aware, so reports from outside the laboratory are essential.

Perusal of the autobiographical literature regarding OOB's is also useful, particularly where it involves talented experimenters. The accounts of Muldoon, Monroe, Lilly, Roberts, Fox and myself come to mind in this connection (see bibliography). It is important to keep in mind that the "limits" discovered by one experimenter may be easily surpassed by another. If we look at the most successful explorations, the chances increase that we will avoid restricting our conceptions of OOB possibilities.

Generalizations about OOB's and those who have them can be drawn up by statistical methods as in any other type of research. We can expect that the most valuable information will come from experienced OOB explorers with a high degree of self-insight who have developed the ability to make precise observations. Hopefully, many more people with OOB experience will take the time to acquaint themselves with the literature and with the OOB's of others, as well as with the potential implications of their particular explorations. There is no need for any specific "training" program developed by research scientists. However, researchers can certainly formulate questions and/or devise experiments for OOB practitioners to try out. Asking better questions is the benchmark of scientific progress in OOB research, but at this point the best questions are likely to come from those outside the old paradigm, particularly the OOB explorers themselves.

Report-gatherers should realize that OOB experimenters have biases of their own which may weight the reports. Since OOB exploration has yet to be accepted on equal footing with other empirical pursuits in the natural and social sciences, OOB explorers are often at pains to legitimize themselves. Non-verifiable or particularly spectacular OOB's probably do not get reported nearly as often as their more conventional counterparts because of this. The explorers realize that the more bizarre the reports sound, the less credible both OOB's and the experimenters become. Consequently, progress in OOB and other kinds of altered awareness research is inhibited.

An OOB explorer with a sound background in the study of altered awareness in general, and paranormal events in particular, is very well-suited for a role as a researcher. Adventure and experiment can be reconciled in OOB studies, though people who are interested in OOB's for the novelty of the experience alone usually lack the persistence to continue experimentation. Events of this type require a new science in which explorers who are experimenter, subject and experiment all combined figure prominently. The traditional values of intellectual sophistication and empirical study of testable hypotheses can be maintained in such studies.

Reading the recommended bibliography may be particularly useful for experimenters. Even if the urge for adventure wins out in the end, and experimentation in any systematic sense seems dull, the background provided by initial acquaintance with these readings should help expand the experiential horizons of the OOB pioneer. Experimentation in its broadest sense has the aim of clarifying our understanding of experience, so even if formal experiments get left behind, the OOB explorer may find the experimentation continuing after all.

Findings and Guidelines

Present findings cannot be considered final, and not only because of the paucity of systematic research. Since the goal of all of this is to expand rather than limit human potentials, any apparent limitation of OOB practice should be assumed to be temporary.

The best guideline for reseachers is to remember the flexibility of the out-of-body state. OOB's do not need to conform to normal space-time laws. The attempt to make them conform can warp the experiences themselves, by imposing unnecessary limits, in addition to producing a lot of wasted experimental time. Present reports, both published and unpublished, indicate the great fluidity of OOB experience. This central fact should be remembered by explorers as much as by the researchers who listen to them.

The greatest impediment to successfully understanding and exploring OOB's is the assumption that they are bound by the same restrictions experienced in the usual waking state. Since we normally assume that movement in space requires time, for example, we are likely to report an episode of instantaneous transition into or out of the body as a "temporary blackout." Celia Green's Institute of Psychophysical Research encountered just this type of description of OOB transition periods among experimental subjects.[1]

Many subjects note that they need not assume a "second body" form. Some, like Lilly[2] and myself,[3] state their belief that the "second body" is a vehicle for integrating OOB information, and that it can be discarded. Reports from other experimenters, who have assumed a variety of OOB forms, including a sphere of light, a point of consciousness and a "bodiless" condition, especially those from subjects with only one recorded OOB, may indicate the absence of tactile sensation rather than actual bodilessness.

Persons who describe classical OOB's usually report the sensation of being fully present in their externalized location. This differs from clairvoyant perception in which the subject can observe a scene from various visual vantage points without the sensation of actual presence at the site.

---

[1]Celia Green, *Out-of-the-Body Experiences* (New York: Ballantine, 1968), p. 133.

[2]John Lilly, *The Center of the Cyclone* (New York: Bantam, 1972), p. 212.

[3]James J. Donahoe, *Dream Reality* (Oakland, CA: Bench Press, rev. ed., 1979), pp. 68-70.

The classical OOB may be considered to be a complete externalization of awareness, while clairvoyance (also called remote viewing) may be classified as a partial extension of one's awareness beyond the usual space-time boundaries. It must be recognized that people will have experiences which are similar to discrete OOB's in some ways and not in others. Though such experiences fall outside our definition of OOB's, their value is not therefore diminished.

It is possible to retain full intellectual acuity while out-of-body along with heightened perceptual capacity involving all the senses. According to the study discussed by Celia Green (and conducted by the Institute of Psychophysical Research), the above characteristics seem to be the rule rather than the exception. OOB reports, like dream records, which show diminished capacity in one or more sensory modalities are common. People who report such reduction of sensation should be asked to detail memories regarding waking state events. It is possible that many of them will report similar reduction of the same sensory modalities in the memory of their waking state experience. In other cases, experimenters out-of-body have found that merely remembering to smell, touch, hear or see is sufficient inducement to restore the absent or reduced sensation to normal or enhanced intensity.

The study conducted by the Institute of Psychophysical Research indicates that "distortions" of OOB perception of the waking state environment occur more frequently in volitionally induced OOB's than in spontaneous ones, for novice practitioners. The tendency to "distort" varies in experienced OOB travellers. If volitional induction of an OOB increases "distortion" for an experimental subject, this would obviously bode poorly for a laboratory investigation of that person. It should also be noted that the interest in OOB/waking state environment overlap differs from person to person. Some prefer to explore presently non-verifiable realms on an exclusive basis. These realms are often tied to the explorer's conception of higher consciousness and considered superior to more mundane excursions for that reason. The merits and disadvantages of such a value judgement require closer examination. Among autobiographical records of extensive OOB exploration, Muldoon's (see bibliography) stands out precisely because of his exclusive preoccupation with waking state locations for his OOB's.

Discarding Waking Limitations

Experimenters report that their OOB capacities increase as their experimentation continues (a learning effect identical to that reported by lucid dreamers). Part of this progress appears as one becomes acclimatized to a situation in which normal space-time laws need not operate. Leaving the body in a "second body" form, with the consequent ability to walk through walls and fly over rooftops, represents a partial transcendence of waking state conventions. The assumption that waking state limitations need to be carried over to OOB travel restricts the experimenter, but it also helps structure OOB's in a familiar fashion. How far any experimenter wants to go beyond the familiar is a matter of personal decision. That it is a matter of decision is an important point. The role of volition is as central for OOB's as it is for psychedelic or dream experience. The fact that this role has been so frequently underemphasized is all the more reason that it be brought to attention here.

The following is a summary of ideas which help to expand the possibilities of the OOB experimenter. How successful people will be in putting these principles to work remains to be determined, as does the relationship of such success to the range of verifiable OOB's.

1) Clear and intense perceptions do not require a physical body form. Unclear understanding of this idea can lead beginners to imagine the OOB as a nebulous experience of rudimentary perceptions. In fact, reports indicate that

OOB experience usually equals or excels the perceptual intensity of the waking state.

OOB's in which people leave in the form of a point of consciousness, ball of light and so on show that a duplicate of the physical form is not required in order to integrate intense perceptual material. Other experiments demonstrate that it is possible to alter one's "second body" form after one is out-of-body.

2) Transference of your location does not require time; it does not require experience of the intervening space (when out-of-body). OOB explorers who try to travel using the conventional model often report a feeling of wind rushing by the face, the sound of wind and the sensation of hurtling through space. They usually report few, if any, additional sensory details. An exception to this occurs when the OOB is a "second body" type flying experience, with the practitioner alternately floating and soaring around, and usually trying to navigate by aerial geography (a notably unsuccessful method of OOB travel). Some OOB experimenters have noted an instantaneous change of location, particularly upon leaving or re-entering the physical body. It seems likely that the sensations of "travel" depend upon the mode selected by the person out-of-body. If someone chooses to operate with somewhat usual space-time conceptions, the OOB state will seem to conform, though at times minimally so.

3) The senses may operate in different ways out-of-body than they do while in the body. Cases of 360-degree vision, synesthesia, and other perceptual alterations have been reported.

4) Your bodily form (physical, "second body," etc.) need not retain constant boundaries. In non-discrete OOB's (discussed in the beginning of this chapter), the subject seems to stretch out beyond normal body boundaries. While out-of-body, it is possible to merge with other beings, experience a "field consciousness" or dissolve bodily form altogether, without losing awareness.

5) Your identity is not limited to your normal person-

ality or even to a single bodily age and form. OOB's have been reported in which the subject experiences being another person with distinct (and different) psychophysical characteristics. In other OOB's, you might experience being several identities simultaneously, perhaps in bodily form, perhaps not.

6) Your perceptions are not limited to a single environmental set. The simultaneous perception of multiple environments can occur during an OOB. More commonly, OOB subjects recall super-impositions of material from "separate" environments, as in a collage composed of your own OOB environment, someone else's dream environment and another person's waking state environment.

7) The experience of time in an OOB is not limited to the usual linear, clock-bound form. OOB's may be _time-dilated_ relative to the clock (an experience of many subjective hours taking only minutes by the waking state clock). The subject may experience an event which comes out of the waking state past, present or future. Finally, an OOB may present waking state past, present and future in seemingly simultaneous form.

8) Your waking state identity and environment are not necessarily the axis of your existence, though they may appear to be, nor are they primary bases from which all perceptions must be evaluated.

9) The OOB (and waking state environment) does not stand as an external "reality" in relation to oneself, in subject-object fashion.

10) The previous two assumptions can be held on eminently rational grounds. Abandoning the old paradigm does not require a repudiation of rational thought and empirical investigation. Of course, it is one thing to make a change of this sort merely intellectually and quite another to accept the implications psychologically.

7

Redefining Death

Death continues to be redefined clinically as the technology for sustaining biological functions advances. Not too long ago, the cessation of heartbeat meant death. Now, resuscitation after cardiac arrest happens every day in hospitals around the country. The current criterion, a flat EEG readout maintained for some minutes, indicates "brain death" to the attentive doctors, though people have been brought back from flat EEG's. Ironically, we turn to machines to determine a person's death and life. What these machines tell us is not any psychological or metaphysical absolute, such as a definitive "death," but merely the limits of our ability to bring someone back to awareness of the consensual "reality" of the waking state, and to the capacity to communicate within the matrix of that awareness. Hospital machinery can keep the rest of the body functioning long after "brain death."

Since the common conception of death is the clinical one, and since "clinical death" is both an evolving definition and a tautologous one (if someone "returns," they weren't dead), technocratic proof of survival after death is impossible; the question of survival is posed in a way which makes its solution untenable. We need to look at an alternative conception of death. The best current evidence for this comes from research in altered states of consciousness and the paranormal.

Altered State Approaches

Altered state events and the paranormal overlap considerably, so some acts, like out-of-body experiences (OOB's), lucid dreaming and mutual dreams will be assigned to their traditional categories here, though each would fit in either of the two.

Some of the major contributions of altered state experiments to a revision of the death concept include the studies of psychedelic experience, mysticism, lucid dreams and near-death returns. These categories are linguistically discrete, though they form a seamless experiential fabric.

Chronicles of death-rebirth experiences occupy a prominent place in the literature of psychedelic exploration. Since the primary facet of death is its experiential, personal part, we can assume that such experiences have something to tell us about biological death as well. We can look at psychedelic death-rebirths as symbolic, but then physiological death is not exempt from the same judgement. People who go through a death-rebirth session often lose their fear of biological death, as do people who experience OOB's. Their change of attitude does not prove that such experiences are identical to biological death, of course, since here again the problem of ''proof'' is set up in unacceptable terms. These experiences do suggest a possible re-routing of the question of what death is.

Mystical experience, whether encouraged by psychedelic ingestion or not, engenders a transcendence of the problem of death. Not everyone comes out with the same answer to the question. This variety suggests that the same may be possible for people who go through biological death; namely, that a number of after-life possibilities may be present. The compulsion to standardize the after-life existence may be a mere atavism dependent upon the high value we give to consensual verification in the waking state.

The major insight of mystical and psychedelic experience (especially where the two intersect) about death is that it is a transformation of consciousness, not an annihilation of it. Whether some continuity of personal memory occurs across the gap, a necessity if "survival of the personality" is to have any meaning, may not be important. Those who have experimented extensively with their dreaming realize the flexibility of one's identity in dreams. The dreamer may inhabit a different body, personality and time period, and even an environment with different space-time "laws," and think nothing is unusual. Dream experimenters, like mystics, realize that one's sense of identity is independent from personality, bodily form and so on. We might suspect that the more experiences someone has which involve alterations of these peripheral aspects of identity, the less death is feared.

With the above context, the usual worries about physical death are bypassed. It is possible to be unafraid of death though, and still interested in what lies beyond it. Different answers, perhaps representing different choices, get repeated by explorers over the centuries: Death is an annihilation of consciousness; death is a merging of personal consciousness with a higher field of awareness (the analogy of the river merging with the ocean); death is a separation from the physical body into a permanent or semi-permanent OOB; death allows a recognition of the "deathless condition," the "One without a second," or primary awareness beyond a self; and so on. All these models represent states of consciousness which can be obtained without clinical death, yet it is interesting that people who return from near-death report experiences similar or identical to the previous descriptions. Possibly the only thing wrong with these depictions of the after-life condition is their exclusivity. A person might have a choice, for example, or experience some combination of the above, or experience a condition not listed.

Paranormal Research

Since the inception of the Society for Psychical Research in both England and the United States in the 1880's, many parapsychologists have looked to the paranormal as a means of demonstrating after-death survival, called the "survival hypothesis" in the literature. The founding members of the SPR had the survival hypothesis as their principal goal, in fact, though later parapsychologists began to emphasize other concerns.

The combination of studies of out-of-body experience (OOB), mediumship (as it applies to communication with the dead), apparitions, mutual dreams and reincarnational memories makes the survival hypothesis a minor shift in thought compared to some of the other implications of such research. The major objection to the survival idea in the parapsychology literature is the "super-ESP" hypothesis and its variations. This latter concept allows for virtual omniscience to be attained by human beings via ESP, thus obtaining all the information which seems to come from the dead. The presumption is that the information only seems to come from the dead, and that this is due to unconscious impersonation or dramatization on the part of the perceiver. Though this idea may help materialists rest more easily, that is the only conservative thing about it. It all depends upon where the investigator wants to put the burden of proof. If we accept the idea that spirits are illusory, we can equally assume the same for beings we meet in the waking state . . . and of course, for ourselves as well.

OOB experimenters report a reduction or elimination of their fear of physical death because they assume that

OOB's demonstrate the independence of identity from physical form. Again, there is no way to prove their assumption by using the model and tools of present technocratic expertise. But this dilemma is the same one confronted by anyone who experiments with his or her own experience. EEG correlates do not prove that dreams exist; for such evidence we depend upon the reports of dreamers. The traditional tools of present-day science arise from a disintegrating world-view. For the new sciences which paranormal and altered state experiences demand, we need to develop an openness to personal experimentation, and a readiness (particularly on the part of explorers) to develop precision of observation and an expanded vocabulary of description. These two factors, along with psychological and intellectual sophistication (as it applies to these realms of study), can provide the base for accumulating and evaluating evidence in scientific fashion.

Mediums operating either in full trance, with a control personality speaking through them, or in a light trance using speech or automatic writing have produced information which only the supposedly communicating dead person would know. The major debate is over how to explain this fact, not whether or not it is true. (Some fascinating "conversations" with spirits conducted by early mediumistic investigators, and the care with which the investigations were made are detailed in references in the bibliography.) Interestingly, mediums have received communications from people purporting to be dead who were alive at the time, or even fictitious creations of the investigator.

Similar anomalies occur throughout paranormal research. Apparitions of the dead have appeared to friends, announcing the event hours before its actual occurrence. In a case of reincarnational memory documented by Ian Stevenson, M.D., one boy came out of a fever with the apparent memories of a man who died during the boy's life. Obviously, our linear conception of time and our simplistic equation of identity with personality and bodily form, are not adequate to deal with these events. The existence of mutual dreams opens the door a little more, since such dreams are consensually verifiable, with a perceptual intensity and coherence that rivals or exceeds that of the waking state. The mutual dream fits all the criteria for a valid, waking state event—except that it does not occur while the participants are awake.

Transitions and Reconciliations

The combined evidence indicates that the world is much more fluid than the conservators of the old paradigm would acknowledge. If we take all the reports, not just the ones which conform strictly to verifiable, parapsychological standards, we see that no aspect of the paranormal provides a clear case for establishing the revised paradigm that traditional parapsychologists want. To be accurate, we need to look at the experimenters' reports in full, and these inevitably include strange intersections of supposed fictions with accurate, parapsychological data. Actually, even with the best psychics, parapsychological performance is unsteady. The mistake traditional investigators make is to assume that this "unsteadiness," like the cases of the fictitious spirit communicator or the odd reincarnational memory mentioned previously, is a flaw. It may very well be the clue to unifying the findings of paranormal and altered state research.

What we end up with after considering all this is the perception of a world in which singularities abound, a world for which there is no determined, fixed shape, whether during life or after death. Suspension of normal consensus beliefs, which is what death of any kind is, means the normal rules are off. The attempt to impose a consensually agreed upon; i.e., definitive and final, structure to the after-life fails in the same way that the technocratic approach does. The question "what is there," so central to the view of the world as separate from the observer, and to the chauvinistic idea that the waking state is the axis of existence, subsides, to be replaced by "what do you want." How we arrange existence gets determined by experiment, as always, a combination of discovery and invention in which the new scientist and new artist are simultaneously the investigators, the experimental subjects and the experiments themselves.

Part III:

Theories

and

Wonders

8

Chance Twists: Synchronicity

Teaching a class on the principle of synchronicity gives the principle itself carte blanche to do what it will, affected somewhat by the shifting moods, inclinations and wishes of both students and teacher. I have taught many graduate classes and seminars which centered upon some aspect of the extra-mundane. In most of these, what emerges is particularly well-suited to the subject matter of the class—strange experiences for the students, reassurances from the teacher that these events aren't so strange when you think about it, and eventually, a 20th century mix of clamoring for spectacles, repeating questions that were answered long ago, miracles (both noticed and unnoticed), triumphs of ''ordinariness,'' and a babbling multitude of conflicting reactions to any given synchronistic event, ranging from contemptuous dismissal to near-reverent gratitude. All of this starts once people begin to dwell on the concept which Carl Jung gave its present name.

Improbable Occurrences

When Jung presents synchronicity as a principle complementary to the idea of causality, he is referring to classical, linear causality. Linear causality implies that event A causes event B, which in turn causes event C, and so on. This model requires a sequential grouping of events in which each event follows the previous in an unbroken, serial fashion. When Jung said that synchronicity operated in "acausal" fashion, he meant that synchronistic events were not explainable in terms of this linear model of causality.

In Jung's introduction to the *I Ching* (Wilhelm translation), he speaks of another concept apart from the idea of linear causality, a Chinese approach which we would now call an ecological or holistic view, which Jung identifies as a synchronistic model of the universe. The *I Ching* suggested to Jung a picture of a universe in which all events interrelate, and in which the connecting factor involved in such relations is *meaning,* rather than linear cause and effect.

Linear cause and effect is, of course, an assumption which works very well for certain kinds of tasks and very poorly, or not at all, for others. The notion of linear causality is similar in many ways to the postulates of Euclidean geometry. Straight lines and plane surfaces may not exist in nature, but assuming their existence works well for all kinds of everyday activities, from carpentry to getting to the grocery store and back. Euclidean postulates do not work very well for getting a man to the moon, however, or shooting a rocket into space. We talk and behave as if there were straight lines, as if there were linear cause and effect, as a matter of convenience, since under many conditions these assumptions can be very useful. What is important about these premises is that they are functional. The natural sciences are built on premises which are functional for certain tasks, however inaccurate these same premises appear when observed from other perspectives.

The Chinese perspective embodied in the *I Ching* looks very similar now to ecological and general systems thought. Linear cause and effect is just too simple a model to use in regard to the world biosphere, to subnuclear physics, to biochemistry, to fields inside and outside the matrix of the natural sciences. Pesticides in the eco-system, the wide ranging effects of a single drug on the workings of the brain, and the complex behavior of "particles" which are also waves are all phenomena which help undermine the linear approach to events. The demise of linear causality means the end of determinism. Possibilities for some kind of predictability and control remain, though predictions must be made in terms of probabilities rather than certainties; the reign of the Uncertainty Principle is upon us, in more ways than one.

The premise underlying synchronicity, and the operation of intuition as well, is that each event is a configuration which will never repeat. When you consult the *I Ching,* the same question repeated on different occasions, even minutes apart, will yield a different answer. The same holds for any means of divination, "divination" being the general name for any attempt to employ synchronicity awareness; i.e., to interpret events by means of imaginative association. With synchronicity, and consequently with intuition as well, change is the "order" of events. Rigidity (redundancy) of interpretation should thus be avoided, since the same symbols can mean quite different things. The *I Ching* itself makes this fact obvious by presenting sixty-four hexagrams to cover all situations.

Each method of divination in common use has disadvantages arising from the cultural framework which produced the method. The *I Ching*'s selection of hexagram titles are fine ones, but the "Images" and "Commentaries" reflect the parochialisms of a feudal, agrarian culture long past. The Waite Tarot is loaded with medieval images of family, battle and religion—again, anachronisms which impede successful interpretation, however much romantic mystery they lend to the process. As you might expect, Aleister Crowley's version of the Tarot revolves around Crowley's obsessions with power and eroticism. And so on.

The concept behind the Tarot is the same as that behind

the *I Ching*, but with an interesting twist. With the Tarot, cards commonly used as a game of *chance* become instruments of prediction—probability inverted into synchronicity. Much of the theory of probability owes its existence and motivation (in legend, at least) to the drive of gamblers compelled to master games of chance. Synchronicity is the "other side" of the idea of chance.

Scrambled Causes

The idea of linear causality has an applicability about as limited as the use of absolute, dual, moral principles, or, what amounts to the same thing, the idea that all phenomena can be reduced to either/or categories: true or false, here or there, worthwhile or worthless, etc. To do without such reasoning completely is impossible, but its indispensability should not be confused with its childlike and childish degree of oversimplification.

The injunction, "do without binary thinking," is an easily misconstrued bit of advice. To use a metaphor from physics, an electron may be unlocateable, and sometimes behave as if it were in two places at once (thus contravening "commonsense" either/or reasoning). However, the electron's strange behavior does not mean it is nowhere at all. Philosophies of negation, like Madhyamika Buddhism (as represented by Nagarjuna) deny causality, deny space-time, and end up with. . . nothing—a justifiable procedure to the faithful in that it demonstrates the inadequacy of all basic philosophical maneuvering, including its own. What the confused and converted aspirants are left with (through use of such a system) is the untenable conviction of their own non-existence—to which the cynic might reply, "If only it were true!" In short, they are left with paradox. Such a philosophical exercise seems to destroy the very supports it stands on, just as did the Surrealist mechanical sculpture which, upon unveiling, proceeded to shift and clank, shedding gears and parts until the whole assemblage had reduced itself to rubble before the bewildered spectators. Madhyamika Buddhism did no more to reduce the practice of philosophizing than the Surrealist sculpture did to end art.

The true irony of examples like these is that they actually perpetuate what they pretend to destroy. One might imagine a whole collection of such things, perhaps in a children's book entitled *Imaginary Beasts*. Chapter 1: ''Philosophies to End All Philosophy'' (Hume, Nagarjuna, etc.), Chapter 2: ''Anti-Art Museum Pieces,'' Chapter 3: ''Zen Rituals,'' Chapter 4: ''Non-Gurus with their Anti-Cults,'' Chapter 5: ''Famous Last Books'' (including *Love's Body* and *Finnegans Wake*), Chapter 6: ''Societies of Anarchists,'' Chapter 7: ''Irrationalist Manifestoes,'' and Chapter 8: ''Evangelists of Scepticism.'' And so on. It gets to be a bit much to get through all those chapter titles, but this is not nearly so painful as the histories themselves.

A *caveat* would have to be inserted somewhere in the forward to the book: ''Whoever acts out these follies without laughing is dangerous; whoever acts on them laughing hard enough does not exist.''

A little humor on these themes, cynical as it may get, is infinitely preferable to the holy-war seriousness typically evoked, or so it seems to me.

''Unthinkable Causes''

Without the operation of a domino-type causality, theoretical certainty wanes to mere probability. This does not end all possibility for prediction or control, but merely reduces and complicates it. Paranormal events can be directed voluntarily to a degree, depending upon the person, the setting and the event. Such events are neither totally predictable and controllable, nor completely outside the province of human volition. When Jung advanced his theory of synchronicity (borrowed from

Kammerer's "law of seriality," as Koestler points out), he intended it to cover the entire range of parapsychological events. Since, by his definition, synchronistic events are "acausal," Jung fails to account for the fact that paranormal events can be induced volitionally. This latter possibility falls under the catch-all hypothesis of "magical causality" according to Jung, and he considers such an explanation untenable because of its "unthinkability." What he meant, of course, is not that "magical causality" was *unthinkable*, but that it was *unpleasant* for him to think about it. Jung feared that the premise of "magical causality" would let in all the ghosts, goblins and superstitions that rationality held at bay. Why not assume, for example, as did an African tribe Jung visited, that performance of a certain ritual keeps the sun coming up each morning? The sun is still rising, isn't it? The answer to Jung's dilemma is a simple one since the possibility that some events can be directed paranormally does not imply the same for all events.

Some paranormal acts may be explained in terms acceptable to the natural sciences; others will not. A paranormal event can be produced volitionally and still be unexplainable within the normal causal matrices of science. To call such an event "pseudo-causal" (as Koestler does in *The Roots of Coincidence*) is somewhat misleading, since this implies that causality must require some physical mechanism. The conscious production of paranormal events presupposes some type of causation, but this need not be interpreted in simplistic, linear terms. A complete approach to the paranormal must include intentionally produced events as well as spontaneous cases, to which must be added more distinctly acausal synchronistic events.

New Meanings

In *The Case of the Midwife Toad*, Arthur Koestler discusses the life and work of Paul Kammerer, the

Austrian biologist who conducted careful and prolonged experimentation (lasting decades) in his attempt to prove that succeeding generations inherit the acquired characteristics of the parents. The interpretation of his results remains controversial, since one of his specimens, the midwife toad, turned out to be doctored. Although the evidence indicates Kammerer played no part in the deception, and though Kammerer himself regarded the midwife toad experiment as inconclusive at best (he performed other experiments which, to his mind, did demonstrate the inheritance of acquired traits in convincing fashion), the scandal raged fiercely enough to result in the scientist's suicide. Critics of Kammerer interpreted his death as an admission of fraud, and to this day history books retain this view. Koestler shows the unfairness of this interpretation.

Though Koestler's presentation of Kammerer's biological work and life story is fascinating enough, my closest attention alighted upon the book's appendix, a study of Kammerer's work on meaningful coincidences. Kammerer kept written records of all sorts of meaningful coincidences and developed a taxonomy of them. His observations appeared in his book entitled *Das Gesetz der Serie* (the law of seriality), which outlined a "law" clearly anticipating Jung's theory of synchronicity.

On first glance, this "appendix" to Kammerer's life seems inexplicable. Why should a biologist completely immersed in countering the Darwinian orthodoxy be at all interested in meaningful coincidences? And why, for that matter, should Koestler include an appendix on Kammerer's study of "seriality" in a book dedicated to the scientist's biological research?

By demonstrating the inheritance of acquired characteristics, Kammerer would prove that, at least in some cases, an organism can pass on what it learns to surviving generations, that a continuity of learning across death is possible on the biological level. What Kammerer gropes for without finding, what Jung half-articulates, and what

Koestler, looking back on both, realizes, is the evolutionary implication of meaningful coincidences. The concept of synchronicity (or "seriality," or whatever term you care to use in this context) describes a principle complementary to the idea of randomness in classical probability theory, a principle which cuts across causality and normal conditions of space-time to produce a meaningful ordering of events. Koestler calls this principle the "Integrative Tendency." This phrase bears a resemblance to what Jung means when he refers to the "transcendent function" operating within the psyche, but Koestler's formulation clarifies the evolutionary movement involved.

Now the connecting link between Kammerer's two preoccupations becomes visible. Evidence for the inheritance of acquired characteristics does for biology what the study of meaningful coincidences can accomplish for psychology (and perhaps physics); namely, it shows that learning takes place on a wide variety of fronts, biological as well as psychological, and that this learning, the integration of newly-acquired meanings, does not limit itself to commonly conceived boundaries.

On the practical level, of course, the question is this: What can participants in a synchronistic event do besides merely identify it as such? By definition, a synchronistic event evokes a greater sense of meaning than simpler forms of coincidence, but this does not solve the problem. If synchronistic events are to serve some evolutionary, developmental process on the personal level, then something more than recognition is required. Newly-acquired meanings indicate the developmental process at work. The danger in the interpreting of synchronicity is the same as in the decoding of dreams: the dreamer can circle around the same stale set of interpretations. If this condition lasts, in all likelihood the dreamer will give up reflecting upon his or her dreams, all sense of discovery from dream contemplation having departed.

Paradoxically, this problem of interpretation grows out

of a misunderstanding of the operation of synchronicity, and of psychological and paranormal events in general. These events are structured by observation and anticipation. If you look at synchronistic events as mere flukes, most likely that is what you will find. To paraphrase an ancient saying: the problem lies in the mind of the beholder—not in the synchronistic events. In some cases, just taking a different approach to synchronicity will help, while in others a more comprehensive step may be crucial—that of increasing your vocabulary of interpretations. Familiarity with a number of divinatory procedures helps up to a point. After that point, *their* vocabularies will lag behind.

Ironic as it may seem, I think the major reason behind the psychological stagnation suffered by people with a restricted sense of meanings is an excessive self-concern on the part of the "victim." This narcissism prevents the person so employed from attending to anything but the recurrence of well-worn, familiar thoughts. A person in this state simply won't listen to the other people and other ideas which would liberate his or her sluggish imaginative abilities.

And for those, sluggish or not, who would play with synchronicity, one last piece of oracular advice: form your questions carefully.

9

Polarities
of
Consciousness

Unconscious Powers

The concept of "the unconscious" implies that there exists within a person a sphere of awareness which, while remaining below the level of conscious access, forms the greater part of the personality and determines, to a great extent, that person's behavior. This subconscious awareness can be affected by many means, accidental or intentional, which in turn result in a change in conscious experience and behavior.

Conditioning may be viewed as an attempt to reach "the unconscious" directly. There are two basic types of conditioning, classical (Pavlovian) and operant (Skinnerian). After a number of occasions in which Pavlov's dogs heard a bell just prior to being given food, the dogs no longer required the food in order to salivate; the sounding of the bell alone was sufficient. This contrasts with operant (Skinnerian) conditioning, a procedure demonstrated when rats learn which bar to press to get a food pellet, or, in another case, which door to avoid in order to bypass an electrified grid.

Both forms of conditioning branch out of the principle of association, an idea which Frazer put forward in *The Golden Bough* as one of the primary bases of magical thinking, and which also underlies the concept of synchronicity.

The fact that conditioning succeeds at all, points out the power of unconscious associations. In order to change habits which are deeply rooted in such associations, it may be necessary to appeal directly to the source, in its own language. The "language" of the unconscious is a language of icons, of what might be called visual juxtapositions, in contrast to the linear series of ideas which we traditionally refer to as logical thought. Conditioning can rightly be regarded as a form of learning, though of the most primitive variety, and such a view allows for a more positive view of what otherwise might be seen exclusively as manipulation of the psyche.

Conditioning accomplishes on a basic psychological level what biofeedback allows on the neurological plane. Control of autonomic physiological functions can be learned to a degree, though until recently such functions were thought to be beyond the reach of conscious control. We now know that an entire range of psychological and paranormal processes can be directed consciously as well; these functions too, were formerly thought to be not only uncontrollable, but even non-existent. These range from acts like lucid dreaming to telepathy. Volitionally induced psychological and paranormal acts represent an expansion of the range of conscious intent. Conditioning demonstrates what might be called unconscious intent, in which a full awareness of the process is usually not present.

Like any talents, inner abilities can be explored in many ways, including creatively cooperating with the larger field of being, out of which springs the "I" that "controls." Naturally, it is also possible to seize inner potentialities with all the power mania and manipulative delight which have undermined this planet and the beings inhabiting it. Manipulative grasping is self-frustrating, as the part inflates itself to become a parody of the whole, and self-destructs in the process. But self-parody and self-annihilation are not the only alternatives, and in any case, to avoid new abilities out of fear of their misuse leads to stasis, not wisdom.

All the extensions of conscious intent, including volitional dreaming and conscious paranormal acts, depend upon broadening your conscious access to previously inaccessible, unknown, unconscious regions. Further, knowledge of one region blends into knowledge of the other. The paranormal merges with the subliminal, which in turn reflects psychodynamic wishes and conflicts, and so on. Certainly, the full range of the natural and social sciences can and should be brought to bear upon these powers of the mind, but as I have tried to make clear, such efforts will be hindered by any attempts by one approach, even that of the natural sciences as a whole, to reduce the findings of all other methods of inquiry to its own paradigm.

Adventurers may be afraid of precisely this kind of comprehensive enterprise, though they need not be, since the ''terrain'' at stake will never be definitively mapped. Paranormal acts, altered states—all these phenomena of the creative imagination form part of the paradigm-transcending capacity of the human mind, and as such cannot be exhausted. New ''anomalies,'' as yet unlabeled, will crop up, just as ''telepathy,'' ''out-of-body experience,'' and ''mutual dreams'' have before. No doubt such events are happening already, perhaps mistakenly lumped together under inappropriate, familiar terms—or perhaps without names at all. To return to the explorer's concern that consciousness research avoid science-prompted routinization, it seems just as likely that official scientific investigation will have the opposite effect; namely, that of enhancing exploration by encouraging discovery (accidental or otherwise) of new methods.

Dominant Polarities

By promoting the term "the unconscious," the psychoanalysts showed something of humanity's invincible desire to bifurcate all phenomena. Gurdjieff once said that few men learn to count past the number two, and considering the history of dualistic thinking, I am inclined to agree with him. To split the psyche into "conscious" contents on one hand, and everything lying outside conscious access on the other, is a transparent trick. How can "the unconscious" be an accurate concept, when it is a region which is defined by what is not? In this light, "the unconscious," like other phrases such as "the unknown" and "chaos" (all three seem like interchangeable terms at times), becomes a childish vulgarization of the great mysteries. The really odd fact about this dichotomization is that it actually can yield helpful information—as a tool, it works.

Researchers who take a close look at the subject of polarities of consciousness find their horizons expanding quickly, since these polarities extend into history, religion, mythology, the structure of language, the physiology of the nervous system, the nature of personality and the characteristics of competing ideologies, to name the most prominent areas this study suggested to me. The polarity which first comes to mind is "the conscious" vs. "the unconscious," set up by psychoanalysis. There are a great many others which could be mentioned, some of which I list below. The major point of this listing is that its elements, though derived from diverse conceptual categories, are often associated together. Why should it be that in psychoanalysis, for example, light, the sun, the right hand, the male principle and individuality are all identified with the conscious side of the psyche, while their opposites are identified with the unconscious? Why, in history, are males the political leaders, to such an extreme degree? Why is such an overwhelmingly large proportion of the human population right-handed? The puzzles grow quickly enough to make it seem that present-day cultural bias is not sufficient to explain the presence of these associated clusters of polarized characteristics. Even if all studies of polarity did nothing more than illuminate cultural parochialism, it would be worthwhile—what better way to go beyond such limitations?

In the list below, I present various groupings as they have been associated traditionally, not as they "must" be associated for all time. In some cases, as in the associational link "masculine-control," the association has pathological forms of enactment. Any person who feels his "masculinity" threatened by situations beyond his immediate control is clearly in trouble. In the chart, association (marked by a dash) does not imply equivalence, nor does polarity (opposing sides of the chart) automatically imply conflict. Unfortunately, the history of humanity demonstrates that such polarities are often the basis for conflict within the personality, within civilization, and even within the nervous system. The interconnections between groupings within each modality (the two modalities are represented by the two sides of the chart) should be readily apparent, though the interconnection should not be misconstrued in a reductionistic fashion. Dominance of the left cerebral hemisphere does not "cause" the higher valuation traditionally given to "history," "the individual," or other categories listed on the left side of the chart, but it clearly parallels that fact.

Categories on the left side of the chart correspond to what has been the dominant value-system of our culture and, not accidentally, to what psychoanalysis associates with the conscious side of the personality. The right side of the chart refers, for the most part, to aspects which psychoanalysis (particularly the Jungian variety) considers to be part of the unconscious. Instead of categorizing the two as "conscious" and "unconscious," I prefer to use the labels "p" and "q," each the mirror image of the other visually, and each potentially a constant, or a variable, in mathematical notation. Stan Gooch, to whom I am indebted for his book *Total Man*,[1] goes into fascinating detail on the relationships of various polarities in mythology, language, culture and many other subjects, including the evolution and physiology of the brain. The similarities in my approach will be evident to the reader of *Total Man*, and though my perspective is not identical to the one Gooch takes in that book, interesting comparisons could be made between my own grouping and his "System A" and "System B."

Polarities Of Consciousness

p-matrix	q-matrix
sun - light - fire	moon - darkness - water
day - "the conscious"	night - "the unconscious"
gold	silver
god (or sky-god)	devil (or earth goddess)
father - king - patriarchy	mother - queen - matriarchy
the masculine - control	the feminine - surrender
right hand	left hand
left cerebral hemisphere	right cerebral hemisphere
cerebrum	cerebellum
virtue - work	ecstasy - play
reason	emotion
the rigid	the yielding

[1]Stan Gooch, *Total Man* (New York: Ballantine, 1972).

analysis - differentiation	intuition - unity
history - fact	myth - fiction
the individual - hero epics	the collective - anonymous or group art
the unique - privacy	the common -sharing
memory - linear time sense	immediate present - cyclical time sense
the city	the countryside
the alphabet	hieroglyph or icon
speech - naming	silence - the ineffable
sight - detachment	touch - immersion
senses divided	synesthesia
formula	paradox
statistical prediction - probability	paranormal abilities - synchronicity
philosophical orthodoxy	mysticism
abstract reasoning	experiential learning
sequential	simultaneous
clear	hidden
waking (base-line) state	altered states of consciousness (alternative perceptions)

Some crucial facts stand out in relation to the two matrices. First, Western civilization traditionally assigns greatest value to those motifs associated with the p-matrix. Second, a tremendous surge of interest in q-matrix functions is currently being felt in Western culture, affecting the scientific and intellectual communities along with masses of people in other vocations. The changing societal roles of women (and the ''feminization'' of men), the widespread exploration of paranormal acts and altered states of consciousness, and the articulated opposition to the dominance of p-matrix themes all illumine facets of the current cultural transformation. The extreme amount of q-matrix emphasis now in evidence indicates the degree of repression formerly in effect.[2] This "return of the repressed," as Freud might call it, exhilarates many but worries others. As usual, those most upset by the paradigm-shift are the guardians of the passing tradition.

Ironically, it takes considerable training *not* to take transformations of this sort in stride. While children seem to go about blithely bending spoons, aluminum strips and other paraphernalia by the use of psychokinesis, a scientist chronicling such feats writes:

> . . . I felt as if the whole framework with which I viewed the world had suddenly been destroyed. I seemed very naked and vulnerable, surrounded by a hostile incomprehensible universe. It was many days before I was able to come to terms with this sensation. Some of my colleagues have even declined to face up to the problem by refusing to attend the demonstrations of such strange phenomena. That is a perfectly understandable position, but one which does not augur well for the future of science.[3]

I suspect his fears are exaggerated, arising largely out of the inevitable blinkers imposed upon him by his formal,

---

[2]The reader can decide whether or not q-matrix dominance has already arrived, if not for the culture as a whole, then for many members of it. For some, lip service to q-matrix values provides a way of avoiding p-matrix development without loss of face. In any case, the announced antagonism to many valuable p-matrix functions, like intellectual discrimination, creates a situation in which p-matrix capacities need the greater emphasis. The problem for the teacher (using the word in a broad sense) consists of how to provide such emphasis in a way which will be heard.

[3]John Taylor, *Superminds* (New York: Warner, 1975), p. 76.

scientific background. Over sixty years ago, Freud fell into similar anxieties. During a conversation with Jung, Freud insisted that his reductionistic "sexual theory" be made into a dogma, to be considered what Freud called "an unshakeable bulwark." When Jung asked, "A bulwark—against what?" Freud replied, "Against the black tide of mud, of occultism."[4] Freud's absolutist sexual dogma has since lost its compelling quality, but European rationality remains afloat.

Developmental Implications

A complete shift from p-matrix to q-matrix dominance would usher in a tyranny of its own, as Gooch points out. Hopefully, the balance can be re-established by according respect to both matrices and by utilizing each, or both, where appropriate. Some tasks require predominant use of one or the other matrix, other accomplishments need the cooperative effort of both sides. Studies of left and right cerebral hemisphere activity have shown this to be true in regard to physiological functions. But it is one thing to form intellectual syntheses of various polarized functions, and quite another to experientially integrate those functions.

Polarities can exist without warfare, though humanity's dealings with a two-sided human nature have been clumsy and often brutal. Denying the two sides accomplishes nothing, obviously. The more common strategy, also a mistake, is the attempt to use one matrix to absorb the other. To some extent, each matrix follows different principles and uses a different language. Thus, "educating the intuitive," though an appealing phrase, is a potentially destructive process. The techniques of "education," as commonly conceived, would be disas-

[4]C.G. Jung, *Memories, Dreams, Reflections* (New York: Vintage, 1973), p. 150.

trous if applied to intuitive realms, becoming a mixture as surreal as the laboratory methods now used to "teach" creativity. The counterpart to analytic learning is experiential understanding; the two are complementary, yet discrete, ways of knowing.

In *Total Man*, Gooch hints at the emergence of a new function, a new awareness, which he calls "System C." Its appearance would mean the liberation of the personality from the competitive struggles between p and q-matrix values. Gooch finds support for the possibility of this evolutionary advance in the theme of the triad. Two triads in particular suggest themselves as preliminary models for Gooch's System C:

| Art | Evolving Consciousness |
| Intellect-Emotion | p-matrix - q-matrix |

I have taken the first directly from Gooch; the second is a paraphrase of his schema in my own terms.

In the first triad mentioned, art represents a harmony of expression which cannot be reduced either to simple emotion or to simple formula. Artistic; that is, metaphoric or iconic thought, is misunderstood by those unacquainted with it. Literalists are apt to judge metaphor as falsehood, since they live in the binary world of journalistic logic where a statement is either true or false, x or not-x. Metaphor can be misconstrued by reducing it to an expression of simple emotional preference by the speaker. So we have at least three dimensions of meaning available in metaphor: the emotional, the intellectual and the artistic. Others could be added, of course, like the paranormal. Lines of poetic prophecy include this additional direction of information. Yeats, with his "Beast slouching toward Bethlehem," comes to mind.

In the second triad, evolving consciousness represents the open-ended continuum of development beyond the normal, and thus indicates aspects which transcend the usual bifurcation of the psyche. Gooch suggests, and I agree, that the new powers of evolving consciousness should be integrated in a multidimensional, developmental context. Psychodynamic integration would form part of this new configuration, as would paranormal abilities and intellectual expansion.

Strategies for Evolving Consciousness

The development of the personality depends to some extent upon the person's capacity to perceive what is lacking. ''Develop your weaker side'' is a Jungian motto for self-development. The first step in doing so is to recognize what your weaker side is. Jungian theory tries to accomplish this by delineating its polarities of masculine and feminine, animus and anima, ''conscious'' (analytic) and ''unconscious'' (intuitive). The same technique can be expanded to those values on and off the polarity groupings I have listed. Today, the ''weaker side'' is more likely to be the p-matrix one, at least among young people interested in the study of consciousness, a reversal of the situation presented several decades ago.

Though it would be foolish to lay out a comprehensive curriculum for self-development, a few directions can be pointed out to advantage. Obviously, whether anyone chooses to follow them is not up to authors or teachers who make it their business to propound such ideas. Perhaps the most valuable result of outlining these strategies comes when the student (who may also be a teacher) recognizes the insights therein as his or her own.

Among the crucial capacities associated with the p-matrix I include the encouragement of literacy and of discriminating analysis. These faculties tie in closely with the ability to focus one's attention across time, to expand one's ''temporal bandwidth,'' as the narrator in Thomas Pynchon's *Gravity's Rainbow* puts it. Students of consciousness are not exempt from the problems attending students of all kinds and all ages these days. Many of them are functionally illiterate, not because they cannot comprehend the individual words in a book, but because they do not have the effective strength of concentration necessary to read them. They have allowed their capacity for attention to atrophy in this respect, though not necessarily in others.

A counterpart to the two above abilities, also related to "temporal bandwidth," is a grasp of historical detail on a personal and collective basis. It sounds fine to "erase your personal history," as Castaneda recommends—who can remember it anyway? But the options should be preserved, the more the better. Being a slave to the present is no better than being shackled to the past; the narrower either becomes, the less there is room to move.

To understand basic psychodynamic principles, and to apply that knowledge to your personal life, seems central to effective p-matrix functioning, if that functioning is going to avoid sabotage from psychosomatic disorders, self-destructive "accidents," and other features of emotional poisoning. Good observation in the "field" clarifies psychological insight more than anything else. This kind of insight is better demonstrated than taught. In addition to that, there are always books, "psychology" as well as fiction.

On the q-matrix side, I include the varieties of experiential learning, from language practice to rehearsals for out-of-body journeys. Some things, like paranormal abilities, require firsthand experience in order to be understood. I have described methods for developing paranormal abilities and special dream types in my book, *Dream Reality*, so I will not repeat them here. Both the paranormal and volitional dreaming constitute major contributions to q-matrix powers and beyond.

The exploration of altered states of consciousness can be advanced by the study of iconic language. "Texts" are everywhere, in everything, waiting to be read, in the content of waking state events no less than in the content of dreams. The psychodynamic interpretation of events is simply one line of elaboration. Dreams are not "symbols," as that word is commonly understood. Dreams are not representations of anything else, though elaborating on them can lead to valuable finds.

Iconic language is a language of gesture and association, an art of association to complement the science of logic. Waking state divination, as in consulting the *I Ching*, uses the same principles as dream interpretation; it just applies them to a different subject. Dream interpretation is divination, a creative act of associational play which depends upon the vocabulary and intent of the interpreter. Norman O. Brown writes, "Every phenomenon is scripture, not alphabetic but hieroglyphic."[5] Is it any wonder that all people receive their needed signs, adapted to their understanding of their needs? Any oracular pursuit makes readers wonder if the meanings are "out there," perhaps provided by some unseen hand. To conclude so brings about a restriction of possible meanings, an unnecessary finality, an ending to the plot. What we need are beginnings, not endings. The Hand that leaves its Signature upon the world is your own.

Transcending the Opposition

The developmental advance which becomes possible when the two matrices cooperate rather than battle may be suggested by the diagrams, or by the label "System C" which Gooch proposes, but it is more accurately described not as a system, but as the experiential transcendence of polarities which normally limit one's perceptions and abilities.

[5]Norman O. Brown, *Closing Time* (New York: Random House, 1973), p. 99.

A description of how I envision this stage may show some of the directions which simultaneously embody it, and allow one to reach it.

The transformation process, the reformulation of somatic and psychic perceptions, forms the most spectacular branch of polarity transcendence. The language of irony, of humor, and of paradox comes into its own. Fluidity of awareness allows for the use of p-matrix and q-matrix values, singly or in unison. What Colin Wilson calls "Faculty X," the ability to perceive meanings in intensified form, appears in greater force. One of the new powers which may be cultivated is the ability to induce ecstatic states.

Evolving consciousness, progressing beyond the polar matrices mentioned, provides the chance for transcending history; this is not accomplished, however, by simply ignoring it. The alterations in space-time perception made available by paranormal actions produce an alternative to the normal way of seeing cause-effect and sequentiality which is far more convincing than the fables in books. Along with the transcendence of previous space-time boundaries comes the abolition of art, in its special sense; this is something artists themselves announced decades ago. Or, what may be more likely, "art" and "science" may remain as terms, while including kinds of activity unenvisioned at present.

Perhaps an early key to this stage lies in a specialized version of what I call the therapy of exhaustion. To play it, you must imagine all the characteristics of liberation you can, in vivid fashion, and then exhaust their fascination as fantasy objects by replaying them until the tape unwinds. The poor chap in the Tarot's 7 of Cups can see all kinds of opportunities ahead. He hasn't taken any of them, though all are within his reach. Perhaps reaching out and grabbing one is too prosaic and definite for his ethereal tastes. But the freedom procured by suspending action and choice indefinitely is an illusory one, a rationalization for incapacity.

Part IV:

Oracles:

Hopes and Fears

10

Fragments
and
Aphorisms

Boundaries of Arbitration

It is time to move beyond dream analysis. Like any work of art, a dream admits to innumerable interpretations. Psychotherapists who interpret dreams have moved from Freud to Jung to Gestalt, leaving the reductionistic bias of those approaches intact. Dreams are thought to be reducible to rather simple psychodynamic statements. When dream theorists of the interpretative school ask what a dream *means*, they expect to hear a final, conclusive statement about the psychodynamic condition of the dreamer. Such naiveté would be ludicrous coming from a literary critic.[1]

---

[1]Psychologists get away with it because dreams, discarded by conventional ''realists,'' end up on the same garbage pile that modern civilization assigns to all the other depths of human experience. This rag and bone shop may be home for artists, but others have laid claim to it. In fact, the psyche has been staked out and sold as decisively as the electromagnetic spectrum, if you believe the ownership certificates. And the first step these ''owners'' take, whatever their profession, is to build a few fences. Any alternative to the traditional science of limits disrupts such proprietary claims.

As I have mentioned elsewhere, a dream can be interpreted psychodynamically, but so can a daydream, the memory of what happened ten minutes ago, or, in what comes to the same result, a story made up on the spot. The interpretation of dreams depends more upon the interpreter's interests than on the specifics of dream content. Dreams are not reducible to analytic interpretations any more than personality is reducible to sexual needs and conflicts. At present, the first misconception exerts the influence once wielded by the second.

Like waking events, dreams are experiences valid in their own right, and can be interpreted or left alone according to the inclination of the perceiver. Looking for psychodynamic insight in dreams can be as useful as looking for it anywhere else. But interpreting a dream does not tell what the dream means any more than Freud's analysis of Da Vinci exhausts and explains the master of Florence. What the dream means is simply itself, any commentary is further elaboration.

The fact that some dream interpretations ''work'' is merely another example of synchronicity. The interpreter chooses the frame of reference, whether psychodynamic, paranormal, aesthetic or otherwise, and not surprisingly, the dream content begins to ''fit'' the framework more and more as the interpreter looks. The same phenomenon occurs to Tarot readers, *I Ching* casters and astrologers.

* * *

Consciousness has no fundamental form or content. Thus, experiments designed to discover the ''base content'' of hypnagogic phenomena, sleep thought processes, and so on, will be unsuccessful. The findings of such experiments will be reflections of the explicit and implicit biases of the experimenter, the protocol and the subject.

* * *

The attempt to discern a hidden kind of language at work in altered states, variously termed ''trance logic,'' ''primary process thinking,'' ''dream logic,'' and the like, comes from a misunderstanding of metaphoric speech. So-called ''dream language'' (all these terms describe the same phenomena) is associational rather than linear and sequential. Metaphoric speech, like that used by Joyce in *Finnegans Wake*, is a condensation of a great deal of information in a space smaller than that allowed by ''everyday,'' journalistic prose. Thus, such speech inevitably contains ambiguity; unambiguous statements belong to the province of commonsense language and thought. Metaphoric language can be looked at as a suspension of logic, or as a form of higher logic, depending upon your orientation. *Finnegans Wake* could not pass as formal history, but then formal history could hardly pass as art.

* * *

The use of the word ''regression'' is an attempt to give ''objective'' authority to the experimenter's value judgements, from which comes the question as to whether mystical experience and other types of alternative perception are ''regressive'' or not. Generally, the adjective ''regressive'' implies that the activity so named is something that one might have done as a child, but should not do as an adult. This labeling comes from the idea that adults have progressed in all the important ways that people can progress since childhood. Actually, most adults have merely learned along very selective and limited lines. Even along those lines, most adult learning reaches steady-state proportions shortly after one embarks upon a ''career.'' Children are learning constantly. Perhaps the word ''regression'' is the adult's revenge upon himself for growing up.

* * *

The idea that there are discrete, self-contained ''states of consciousness'' can create misunderstandings, particularly when researchers assume that they will be able to find one set of laws which govern LSD consciousness, for example, another set for *kundalini* experience, still another for out-of-body travel, and so on. All kinds of arrangements are possible once you leave waking consciousness behind, but these arrangements are *ad hoc* ones, not the seemingly solid, fixed events and territory of waking awareness. Since for some people the waking state is ephemeral enough, a few excursions into alternative perceptions are sufficient to make a System seem like an attractive security option. That is the only place such security will be found, though, and as always, the walls that keep the bogeymen out also keep you locked in.

Where waking state consensus ceases, rules get suspended. But, fluidity of consciousness being what it is, you can arrange a seemingly stable "environment" of alternate perceptions as well. A mutual dream is one such environment.

The "nonstate paradigm" has already been applied to one area, "hypnosis." Theodore Barber and his colleagues deny the existence of a "hypnotic state," with convincing research evidence to back up their position. A central point is that the act of defining a procedure as "hypnosis" automatically evokes certain expectations in the mind of the subject. The induction procedure adds to these expectations. Thus, for years "hypnotized" subjects felt and looked sleepy, and upon return to normal, forgot what had happened. Now, experimenters have found that age-regression, anesthesia and other abilities formerly credited to the "hypnotic state" can be evoked with simple suggestion, and without a "trance" induction. Further, these subjects can be fully alert the entire time (unless suggestions are formulated to oppostie effect) and remember everything that went on. Barber now refers to his "hypnosis" experiments as exercises in "creative imagination," the latter being both a more positive and a more accurate term.

These exercises in "creative imagination" are also exercises in the subject's capacity to perceive meanings. Thus, patients undergoing desensitization treatment improve when told the procedure is "therapy," and stay the same when told it's all an exercise in "imagination."[2] Learning conscious intent, the ability to pattern events in ways which will be creative and constructive, is the central developmental process involved in the varieties of consciousness, including paranormal, waking and altered perceptions.

* * *

The simplest conclusion to draw about the mutual dream environment is that it consists of consciousness alone, with dream space-time and dramatic events existing as imaginative constructs, subject to "instantaneous" revision. The dream need not occupy space in the usual sense of the term. Interestingly enough, these descriptions of the mutual dreamscape also fit various alternative views of the *waking state* environment (the "life is your dream" idea, for example).

If we apply the criteria of waking state validity (consensual verification, perceptual intensity, etc.) to a dream, and the dream passes the tests, then there is every reason to conclude that the search for solutions to fundamental questions about the nature of the universe cannot be restricted to examining the waking state alone. Thought of this sort represents a progression beyond the waking state chauvinism which underlies the "realism" of present-day materialists. This progression is perfectly consistent with logical reasoning and with scientific (i.e., empirical) investigation. In fact, it forms an appropriate parallel to some of the major transitions applauded by contemporary scientists, like the move from pre-Copernican cosmology to heliocentrism.

If the earth has been de-throned as the center of the

[2]See Nicholas P. Spanos and Theodore X. Barber, "Behavior Modification and Hypnosis," *Progress in Behavior Modification*, Vol. 3, ed. M. Hersen, et al. (New York: Academic Press, 1976), pp. 1-44.

solar system, and man as the center of the universe, then surely the next step is to disavow the sovereign status of the waking state. At each stage, what humanity loses in pride, it gains back in understanding. And perhaps, as this discovery deepens, we will find ourselves on the edge of an even larger step: new recognition of the primacy of the imagination.

* * *

The traps of laboratory research include the search for "final" physiological criteria by which subjective events may be described, compared, and understood. Most of a person's experience is not demonstrable; the experimenter must take the subject's word for it. That you are experiencing pain is no more provable than the fact that you remember (or don't remember) a dream you had last night. Establishing physiological correlates does nothing to lessen the essential uncertainty of such a situation.

Researchers associate rapid eye movement (REM) with dreaming, for example, because subjects awakened during REM describe dreams more frequently than those wakened in non-REM periods. The ultimate factor which determines whether or not we believe subjects are dreaming is what they tell us, not what their EEG registers. More than that, the criteria for a dream, or an out-of-body experience, or pain, or pleasure, are essentially personal, and thus ambiguous and variant.

The illusory precision of defining such experiences physiologically becomes a hindrance when exceptional events are reported. Lucid dreams were ignored for over a hundred years, in spite of the Marquis de Saint-Hervey's experimentation with them, because "lucidity" (in the special sense of the word) and "dreaming" were pronounced contradictory, and lucid dreams declared impossible.

An analogous situation might happen today, with some subject's dream experience pronounced invalid because she failed to show proper dream EEG tracings.

If lexicographers can admit that dictionaries record usage, not legislate it, then perhaps students of consciousness can see through their own definitions and be ready to chronicle the larger possibilities of human awareness.

* * *

No one should be surprised that such similar reports exist for near-death encounters as for out-of-body experience, psychedelic ingestion, sensory isolation and dreams. All these areas exemplify the powers of the human imagination—and imagination is not a "state," but an activity. The categories I have just mentioned are methods rather than results. The same principles apply to imagination *anywhere*, including the waking state. Normal consciousness depends upon an immense concentration on certain sensations, expectations and beliefs.[3]

Guided imagination creates the waking state as it does any altered state. The next revolution in psychology arrives when researchers realize that there is no ontological difference between the waking state and any other "state," and that, to be more precise, the "waking state" does not exist as a fixed, discrete entity, any more than does the "hypnotic state." What you see in a dream, out-of-body, or wherever, is as valid as what you see usually. It's what you do with it that counts.

* * *

[3]Simple introspection can evoke experiences thought to be the province of "altered states of consciousness." In one experiment, researchers had a group look at a point on a wall and merely attend to perceptual changes for ten minutes. The subjects reported a variety of different sensations, including alterations in perceived body shape and size, fluctuations in the color, depth, etc. of the room and sensations of tingling going up the spine. See the following report: Harry T. Hunt, Ph.D. and Cara M. Chefurka, "A Test of the Psychedelic Model of Altered States of Consciousness," *Archives of General Psychiatry*, Vol. 33, July 1976, pp. 867-876.

Celia Green has said, "It is superfluous to be humble on one's own behalf; so many people are willing to do it for one."[4] Likewise, there is no need to talk oneself into further believing the "limitations" of life as a human being. For each description of transcendence of such limits, there are a hundred reassertions that transcendence is impossible.

* * *

A common mistake for explorers of dreams, out-of-body experience and the like is to generalize from their own supposed limitations. Ouspensky writes of the "impossibility" of pronouncing your own name in a dream without waking up. (I had no difficulty performing this feat on the several occasions I tried it.) Spiritualistic out-of-body enthusiasts declare the "necessity" of a "second body" in out-of-body travel. Swedenborg describes having witnessed Mohammedans in the afterlife convert to Christianity, a precondition, he says, for their entrance into heaven. Such reasoning is peculiarly similar to that used in the natural sciences, in which newly observed phenomena are described in terms of preconceived limits. If a traditional physicist finds a person with psychokinetic ability, the scientist tries to find out what the subject cannot move: what materials, how much, under what circumstances. Although this may be sufficiently illuminating from a statistical point of view, it is unfortunately worth very little for expanding individual capacity. If someone tells you that she cannot do something, like float across the room by willing to do so, you may have learned something. . . about her.

Unfortunately, for many people a belief in limits forms a kind of religion. Their set of ideas about the world and about what is possible for them to experience consists of little more than a collection of these definitions of

---

[4]Celia Green, *The Decline and Fall of Science* (Oxford, England: Institute of Psychophysical Research, 1976), p. 4.

limitation. For them, knowledge consists of knowing your menial place in the scheme of things.

Generalizing from your experiences of transcending supposed limits at least provides hope to those interested in moving beyond the established sense of the ordinary.

Aphorisms and Epitaphs [5]

While archaic philosophers are trying to keep mind and body apart, we struggling teachers are trying to keep them together.

* * *

The Circular Definition of Knowledge

The more information that is condensed in any verbal communication, the more ambiguous the communication becomes. One might imagine attempting to convey final, absolute knowledge in a single communication, the amount of information increasing continually, parallel with the rise of ambiguity, until the apex is reached: a message of complete nonsense. So it is said correctly that at the height of wisdom, one becomes again a fool.

* * *

If people criticize themselves, believe them.

* * *

People look to a democratization of art. Everyone wants to become a famous artist, or barring that, at least famous.

* * *

[5] In one discipline of self-development, the reason for giving someone his or her "epitaph" is to intensify recognition of the personality weakness it represents. The trait may persist for a lifetime, but through conscious intent it can be transformed into somewhat of a beneficent factor. Recurring awareness of the trait then acts as a stimulus for strengthening that person's "weaker side."

The trouble with bureaucratic nightmares is that the only solutions are bureaucratic ones.

* * *

Writers, however mystical, who emphasize the place of suffering in transpersonal experience, represent the last gasp of a moribund tradition.

* * *

If you couldn't imagine a better world, there wouldn't be much to your imagination.

* * *

The major difference between a genius and an ordinary person is that a genius knows that he is one.

* * *

Mystical experience, once understood, annihilates mysticism; philosophy, correctly practiced, abolishes philosophy; and history, given enough time, disappears. All these propositions are borne out by this aphorism, which very shortly will vanish from memory without a trace.

* * *

One of the greatest tragedies of modern civilization: the tragic view of life.

* * *

To a person who wants to be unique, all the people in the world are bad examples.

* * *

Quote from a garment tag: "This fabric has been scientifically laundered. Flaws and imperfections are part of the total desired look."

* * *

Hell: Weapon of the unhappy in their fight against heaven.

Moralistic Objections: The trump card of irrationality.

* * *

A terrible, though tempting fate: to have one's writing in every library, in every home, in everyone's thoughts; in short, to have savagely loosed upon the world. . .a pet.

* * *

He refused to let the absence of thoughts interfere with his personality.

* * *

No matter how much a person tries to define himself by what he is not, to find him, look for what draws his enthusiasm. And if nothing comes into view. . .

* * *

He mistook differentiating for distinguishing himself.

* * *

Learn history in order to dispense with it.

* * *

To see yourself as a character in an archetypal drama can be exciting enough, but you're still using someone else's script.

* * *

The disease of psychoanalysis: the tendency to see everything in terms of the past, and not much of a past at that.

* * *

Anticipated Graffiti

One man's infinity is another man's nutshell.
Exobiologists Unite!

* * *

Sex: Humanity's natural urge to make a fool of itself.

Newsquote from a radio broadcast: "Among those asking that the committee keep secret its findings on assassination plots was an anonymous man who said he feared revenge from unnamed sources."

* * *

Western civilization is in the position of a senile man: the loss of its faculties prevents it from realizing it's lost them.

* * *

The only thing worse than searching for a final revelation is finding one.

* * *

The reason that the future seems to turn out no better than the past is this: the requisite difficulty of transforming the ideal into the manifest. As with poetry in a foreign language, so with ideals: the loss is in the translation.

* * *

Let my consumers produce an image of me worthy of their appetites.

11

Transformation

Most systems of self-development[1] aim toward the transformation of the practitioner. How far-reaching this metamorphosis goes depends in part upon the system. Systems which concentrate upon psychotherapeutic results can rearrange the personality in significant ways without producing much in the way of spectacular altered states of consciousness (ASC's) or paranormal experience. Other disciplines focus upon more unusual facets of transformation: visions, ecstasies, spontaneous restructuring of the body, and awakening of paranormal perception. Sometimes these effects arise, along with dramatic tactile sensations which vary in duration from a few moments to weeks. Again, the experiential facets of any transformation process depend to some extent upon the system (if any) the practitioner utilizes. The more unusual events, including physiological effects, will be interpreted according to the theoretical or philosophical biases of the experimenter.

[1]By "systems of self-development" I mean "patented" methodologies like psychoanalysis, Psychosynthesis, yoga systems, Gurdjieffian schools, etc.

One of the more interesting types of transformation is the spontaneous kind which happens without the expectation, and sometimes without the desire, of the person thus visited. The traditional Hindu literature of *kundalini* experience, for example, contains many in stances of spontaneous and unwilled self-transformation. Accounts of transformative experience, including *kundalini*, share striking similarities, particularly with regard to the somatic effects. The cross-cultural parallels include bodily sensations of heat (often localized in the lower back), tingling and vibrating sensations in various parts of the body (often euphoria-inducing), periods of extreme psychological detachment from environmental impressions, tremendous increases in vitality lasting days or weeks (on occasion reducing the apparent need for sleep and food), and ecstatic states which often last for hours at a time.

Some or all of these things may occur to people who undergo transformation, but of course people in such a position do not need this list to validate the fact that they are indeed going through important changes. What a list like this does is to help a person distinguish what could be the byproducts of transformation from psychological or physiological disorders.[2]

The commonality of some of the side-effects of the transformation process, regardless of who experiences it, is certainly intriguing, but to conclude that this "proves" that transformation across the globe is fundamentally the same process would be misleading. One of the attributes of this kind of transformation is the feeling that the experience is meaningful in a transcendent, archetypal way. It becomes easy, once you have undergone such experiences, to take this feeling a step further and assume, mistakenly, that your own experience is the

[2]For a study of physiological events which can accompany *kundalini* experience see: Lee Sannella, *Kundalini: Psychosis or Transcendence?* (San Francisco: Sannella, 1976).

essence of transformation itself, while the variations played out by other people are "incomplete versions" or "distortions" of your own transformation process. Practitioners of *kundalini*, like Gopi Krishna and Swami Muktananda, routinely illustrate this error by assuming that all forms of creativity are really disguised manifestations of *kundalini*.

Though some find maps of transformation encouraging and supportive, thanks to the stamp of consensual "validation" such systems provide, it seems to me that these people lose a great deal of the potential creativity and uniqueness available within varieties of the transformation process. Narratives of transformation experience, like stories of other miraculous events, can be recited to shore up or undermine any given system of self-development. But the major point in talking about transformation, whether this consists of telling miracle stories or of generating theoretical speculation, is to present the powerful fact of transformation itself. It can be explored outside the presently emerging orthodoxies of self-development as easily, if not more easily, than from inside them.

Personal Encounters

The following stories illustrate some of the sublime and ironic perspectives which transformation presents. I participate in most of the events which follow, often as an observer and occasionally as an active, if sometimes reluctant, subject. Most of the direct movement of transformation occurs to Pam Yellen.

She begins:

One evening I indulged in a former favorite mundane pastime—pinball. I moved to press the reset button, setting up another game. Just as my thumb connected with the button, some kind of circuit completed, sending a bone-jarring electric shock through both my arms and knocking me several feet back from the machine. The shock left me dazed and spacey. I warned the manager of his potentially lethal machine and I left. The dazed feelings persisted, along with the aching in my bones, for the rest of the evening. By the next day I felt myself on the verge of a breakthrough in consciousness, a transformation which would enable me to bring on certain psychic perceptions and ecstatic states at will and which would give me the ability to transmit this increased capacity to others.

Strange things began to happen the day after the shock. Although Pam joked about the irony of having an electric shock initiate a transformation (she laughed over the fuel such a fact would give to reductionistic "explanations" of the awakening of paranormal abilities), she could not ignore the strong manifestations which followed:

I began to experience a whole group of intriguing events: sensations of heat spreading throughout my body, often becoming localized in my solar plexus; currents of incredible, ecstatic feelings engulfing my normal consciousness; and occasional feelings of being detached from my body accompanied by a shift in my visual field. When I felt this peculiar sense of detachment, I seemed to be observing the environment from a point above and behind my head. Sometimes these things would occur simultaneously, sometimes separately, but usually lasting several hours at a time.

Pam's familiarity with paranormal and ASC experience allowed her to accept this explosion of inner activity without fear. As a result, none of her experiences felt unpleasant. In fact, according to her, *all* of them felt like a "great improvement over normal waking consciousness." Incidents like the ones mentioned above continued sporadically for several weeks, occupying most of her waking state time.

The predominant feature of this several-week period seemed to be the periods of ecstatic experience in which

Pam felt her intuitive powers operate at an accelerated speed. These ecstatic states came on spontaneously for the most part, but Pam found herself able to induce them intentionally as well. Some of these experiences followed contemporary descriptions of *kundalini*, with an intense sensation of heat rising from the base of her spine to the crown of her head, and then moving from there down to her solar plexus. At times the current stopped at her head, engulfing her head in waves of euphoric vibration. Ecstatic sensations inevitably accompanied the feelings of heat, though occasionally the ecstatic current appeared without any alteration of temperature perception. Sometimes the current stopped descending at the level of her chest and spread out from there to fill her entire body.

I spoke with Pam quite frequently as this series unfolded. If anything, her ability to do "ordinary" tasks increased during this period overall, although she did find herself disinclined to speak during those times she found herself completely immersed in the ecstatic current—a preference which is quite understandable to anyone who has undergone analogous alterations in awareness.

A few times, her ecstatic states produced visible physiological signs. I tried to play "scientific observer" whenever possible, but not to the point of interfering with the process. Here is her description of a few of the times when physiological events accompanied the ecstatic process:

One evening I was talking with some friends when all of a sudden the entire top half of my body became very hot—a burning and itching sensation combined. The sensation came together with a strong alteration in my state of consciousness. I wondered for a moment if I was having an allergic reaction. I looked down at my arms and stomach and noticed a definite rash, which my friends could see as well. The rash extended over my shoulders and back, down both arms and over my chest and stomach. It stayed for about 15 minutes, while the sensation of heat continued. Then, abruptly, these symptoms stopped and I entered an ecstatic state which lasted the rest of the evening.

Several times during my encounters with the heat sensations, other people present could feel heat radiating from my body just by putting a hand near the area where the heat felt strongest to me. This heat usually emanated from the base of my spine or the area of my solar plexus.

The changes in Pam's consciousness over the several weeks involved in her transformation brought in paranormal perceptions as well as these ecstatic states. Although in practice, paranormal cognition can easily blend into ASC experience, making it difficult to distinguish between the two, Pam did pick up verifiable paranormal information on a number of occasions. Since this happens to her in her normal waking state anyway, we have to rely on her judgment to determine how much the psychic perceptions were actually a consequence of this intensive developmental period. About this she remarks:

I did have a greater degree of intuitive awareness during this time, particularly in regard to the internal states of people around me. Normally, I make a deliberate effort to pick up psychic information, when that's what I want to do. But during my transformation I felt I was in continuous psychic contact with nearby friends and acquaintances. I felt automatically aware of what was going on, often to the point of being able to observe another person's stream of consciousness in minute detail, and to verify specific items on the spot.

One of the most dramatic manifestations of Pam's new-found states and abilities came out when she tried to transmit ecstatic states to others. Though a sceptic would be hard put to believe that any "transmission" takes place in such instances, believing rather that the whole process depends upon set and setting, my own conviction is that in some cases ecstatic states can, in fact, be induced in one person by another purely by paranormal means. I say "in some cases" since the experimenter-researcher should not discard the "set and setting" model entirely, but rather allow for the possibility of additional, contributing factors. Like telepathy, transmission of this sort is a highly intuitive field, and is thus not easily divided into manageable variables. I am a biased observer, of course, as are all observers, and here is one of the experiments which helped bring that bias forth:

Pam found that she could transmit ecstatic states similar to her own most easily when she felt particularly energetic. At the moment, I was a perfect candidate. She felt energized, I felt sullen, oppressed by a host of vague complaints and minor physical aches and pains, and reluctant to even let her try to help me pull out of it. As soon as I consented, she concentrated, and within seconds I felt waves of energy moving up my body to disperse my bad temper. I felt myself first holding on to the bad mood, then laughed as I recognized the absurdity of the effort. Immediately, my problems disappeared, and I floated into a very high, energetic state.

I could see the benefits of applying such a power widely, and, in my case, asking Pam for similar bursts whenever the occasion demanded—which would be frequently, I was sure.

"Why don't you transform yourself?" she replied.

Structural Transformation

Psychological transformation, however profound, is one thing, but actual *physical* restructuring is quite another. While other aspects of the transformation process fascinated and intrigued me, this one sometimes made me nervous. Pam moved as easily through this phase as she had the others, although she too wondered what the results would be. But I will backtrack a bit, and let Pam again take up the story.

At the beginning of the transformation, the day after the shock, I felt that part of it would involve a change in my body, but I wasn't sure what that change would be. I thought that my molecular structure would become less rigid and that I would be able to alter it more easily than before. My body did feel lighter and more fluid than usual.

At the height of the transformation, my face seemed to change in appearance. I could feel my cheekbones becoming less prominent, the lower part of my face near my chin thinning out, and my forehead expanding slightly outward in rounded form. Although I had told no one about these changes, less than a week after their occurrence, three of my friends each told me separately that they noticed these specific differences in my face.

This particular part of the transformation took about a week. My face still looks as it did at the end of that week.

Pam thought that physical changes "literalized" her transformation, allowing her to experience a full fluidity of consciousness rather than a "mere" psychological form of transformation. She wasn't sure how pronounced the changes would be, or even whether or not the changes were necessary at all. I was one of the people who noticed the differences in her face, and with typical experimenter's enthusiasm convinced Pam to sit for some photographs which I took in an attempt to document the fact that these were actual physiological changes, possibly in the bone structure itself. I gave up on the project soon, partly because of my rudimentary ability with a camera, but mainly because by the time I began photographing, the changes had already happened. I consoled myself with the thought that physical documentation was probably not that important in this case anyway, since the experiential alterations were the crucial ones; and I think, looking back, that this was correct.

Since I still thought that ecstasy induction was just what I needed, I decided to take Pam up on her advice. . .so I asked her to see if she could use her powers to get me started in the direction of acquiring them myself. This was a rather lazy way to self-development, I admit, even though it *was* formulated as an experiment.

Right away I felt a lot of resistance, as before, to the induction itself, and I had little success working on my own. Then a breakthrough of sorts came about, with an unexpected addition: physical changes.

Some days after my work with transformation started, I felt odd sensations in my forehead, as if it were swelling slightly in size, just above my eyebrows. These sensations came on suddenly, lasted several minutes at most and then disappeared. By about the third time, I felt a buzzing vibration localized above my left eyebrow, accompanied by the distinct sensation that my forehead was beginning to bulge slightly there. I could feel the bulge, and when I walked into the bathroom to look into the mirror, I could see it clearly as well. As with Pam, several friends noticed the change without my mentioning it to them. [Others recognized it once it was pointed out to them.] The total change was small, but distinct and noticeable, at least to me and a few others.

The next time the sensations came on I tried intentionally to stop them and it worked. I had thought about it and concluded that the major point of such physical change was to illustrate that there wasn't any significant difference between ''psychological'' and ''physiological'' aspects of transformation—that the duality of ''mind'' and ''body'' was a false one, and that the transformation process could affect physiological processes, if necessary, to demonstrate the fluidity of even the most ''solid'' parts of the universe as perceived in the waking state.

I still have the formation above my eyebrows.

It appears that even this drastic aspect of transformation has occurred to other people. Dr. Stephen Arnold, a friend of both Pam and myself who is a pioneer researcher in developmental psychology, told me about some changes he underwent some years ago. At the time, he realized his forehead had changed, forming what he humorously calls a "simian ridge," quite pronounced and easily visible. He checked back on photographs of himself as late as his senior year in high school; these showed no ridge at all.

Further Experiments

Since these original introductions to transformation, neither Pam nor I have gone into teaching transformation full-time, but we have conducted a lot of experiments. Some of the results can be summarized as follows: The ability to induce ecstatic states in oneself and others by paranormal means *can* be cultivated, but the continuation of such states on a long-term basis requires bypassing some strong psychological obstacles. One of these is "normal" inertia, another is the difficulty of adjusting, after the process, interpersonal relationships that were in existence before the transformation began. Prolonging any high state of consciousness to the degree that it occupies most of what would normally be waking state time presents problems of its own, including the temptation to dichotomize your high and "normal" states of consciousness, contemptuously disregarding both manifestations of the latter, and people engrossed by the same. However, these problems can be obviated by more compassionate and "ordinary" psychodynamic talents. Enough of the problems.

Transformation presents open-ended developments of identity which remain uncharted. One aspect of the particular direction Pam took in her transformation process involves cultivating the ability to induce ecstatic states. But there is more going on in these states than simple euphoria; they provide a base camp which can enable explorers to move on to all sorts of altered state, paranormal and other talents. The opening of consciousness which is induced by transformation has both ecstatic and developmental components. Learning how to induce ecstatic states, both in yourself and in others, is one possible line of development, but not the only one.

The transformation process, ASC's and paranormal events can be studied as part of the same continuum. The continuum itself offers profound possibilities for exploration. And, if ASC's and the paranormal are to be more than mere curiosities, then some kind of developmental context must be pursued. I am not suggesting any specific model of transformation—in fact, I prefer the opposite. Let each person develop his or her own model, and discard it when the time is right.

Glossary

conscious intent—the use of imagination and will (often in a receptive, relaxed and alert fashion) in order to directly affect psychological and/or physical processes. The concept of conscious intent is an extension of the idea of aware self-suggestion described in the literature on hypnosis. Conscious intent originates within oneself with full awareness of the process.

creative dreaming—the conscious use of the dream state, including the modification of dream content, for artistic and psychotherapeutic creativity.

high dream—a dream in which the dreamer experiences an expanded, altered state of consciousness analogous to psychedelic experience. In many cases this occurs when the dreamer dreams of ingesting a psychedelic.

hypnagogic state—the state of reverie which one enters in the initial stages of falling asleep. This state can consist of partial dreams, very short in duration, or a stream of images, sounds and/or thoughts. It is possible to remain fully conscious while in the hypnagogic state and to exert some control over its content. This conscious use of the hypnagogic state is directly comparable to the conscious use of the dream state which lucid dreaming makes available.

hypnopompic state—the state of reverie one encounters in the process of waking up.

lucid dream—a dream in which the dreamer is aware that he or she is dreaming. Thus, the term "lucid" in this context refers to more than "vivid" or "clear" dream content. Dream lucidity can be induced experimentally. When the lucidity is prolonged enough, the dreamer can then work directly with dream events, while the dream is occurring, rather than waiting to wake up before working with the dream.

mutual dream—a dream in which two or more people share the same dream plot and environment. There are two types of mutual dreaming. In the first, two or more people have the same dream, but without each being present in the other's dream plot. In the second type, at least two people participate in the same dream and are aware of each other's presence. This latter type shows how a dream can have all the perceptual intensity and consensual verifiability of a waking state event. Mutual dreams thus demonstrate the absurdity of asking whether or not an event is "real." What people are usually trying to find out when they ask if something is "real" or not is whether the event in dispute is consensually verifiable.

out-of-body experience (OOB)—an OOB is the experience of moving outside the physical body, with the consequent ability to perceive from a space-time position different from the location of the physical body. The person who "travels" out-of-body feels present in the new location.

People leaving the body may experience moving out in a "second body" form. This "second body" is similar to the physical body in sensation and appearance, as far as the explorer is concerned. While occupying the "second body" form, the OOB traveler can move through solid objects, fly, and alter in size and shape. However, some researchers, including myself, believe the "second body" to be an imaginative construct, manufactured out of the need for familiarity in the midst of unfamiliar circumstances. The fact that some people leave the body in the form of a sphere of light, or a point of consciousness, seems to support this contention.

An OOB "visit" may or may not produce accurate sensory details about the place visited. OOB travels can combine accurate perceptions (from the waking state viewpoint) along with inaccurate ones. Other OOB's take place in environments which do not appear to exist in normal, waking state space-time. "Extramundane" travels of this sort present an interesting puzzle for the researcher, since such travels cannot be verified using normal waking state means.

paranormal event—one of a class of phenomena which includes telepathy, precognition, mutual dreams and verifiable out-of-body experiences. In this book, I use the words "paranormal," "parapsychological" and "psychic" interchangeably.

precognitive dream—a dream which anticipates the future, sometimes to the extent of duplicating exactly the foretold event(s). Precognitive dreams, like their telepathic counterparts, usually have a mixture of paranormal and other kinds of dream perception. Sometimes, precognitive information can be found by "dream interpretation;" i.e., using your powers of imagination to associate elements of the dream with potential waking state futures.

psychokinesis (PK)—the act of affecting physical processes outside one's own body by using the focus of one's awareness, unaided by muscular exertion or other normal means. Poltergeist phenomena, in which objects topple from tables, etc., are thought to be produced by unconscious PK, usually emanating from a single person.

telepathic dream—a dream which contains paranormal information regarding the waking state of someone other than the dreamer.

Annotated Bibliography

Note: It would take volumes to list all the significant books which I have found helpful in exploring psychology's frontiers. Anyone who reads the works described here will have a good grounding in the consciousness research literature, though not an exhaustive familiarity with it.

Many of the books in this section lie outside what readers may be accustomed to regard as psychology or parapsychology, which is as it should be, since the formal works in these disciplines represent only part of the knowledge necessary to the serious explorer. In these regions, over-specialization is a greater danger than eclecticism. For a boundary-transcending subject, an interdisciplinary approach is best. And one of the major points of my discussion is that the idea of what disciplines belong in such an approach should be broadened.

My apologies go to authors who feel their works have been omitted unfairly from this list.

The insatiable reader whose appetite for the written word exceeds the provisions of this listing should be pleased by the large bibliographies to be found in many of the books mentioned.

The bibliography is divided into the following sections: "Autobiography and Biography," "Disciplines of Self-

Development," "Dreams and Sleep," "Fiction," "Historical Intersections," "Out-of-the-Body Experiences," "Paradigms in Transition," "Parapsychological Information," "Psychological Perspectives," and "Visions and Commentaries."

Autobiography and Biography

Bennett, John G., *Witness: The Autobiography of John G. Bennett*. Tucson, AZ: Omen Press, 1974. Bennett studied with both Gurdjieff and Ouspensky and became a teacher himself, one of the most prominent of the Gurdjieff-Ouspensky approach.

Crowley, Aleister, *The Confessions of Aleister Crowley: An Autohagiography*, John Symonds and Kenneth Grant, eds. New York: Bantam, 1969. The explorations of a major figure in the occult tradition who used drugs and ritual sex in his attempt to fuse European magic and Asian mysticism.

__________, *The Magical Record of the Beast 666: The Diaries of Aleister Crowley, 1914-1920*, John Symonds and Kenneth Grant, eds. Montreal: Next Step Publications, 1972. A record of Crowley's sex magick (his spelling), illuminations, *I Ching* castings and assorted other psychic alterations, with notes from the editors to clarify some of the coded terminology.

French, Peter J., *John Dee: The World of an Elizabethan Magus*. London: Routledge & Kegan Paul, 1972. French emphasizes the historical and philosophical place of Dee and his contemporaries, and shows Dee's significance as a scientific, as well as Hermetic, investigator. This book, along with the writings of Frances Yates, forms part of a radical re-examination of Renaissance tradition.

Garrett, Eileen J., *Many Voices: The Autobiography of a Medium*. New York: Dell, 1968. The paranormal experiences and experiments which Eileen Garrett underwent did not affect her analytical, at times sceptical, attitude to the nature of psychic phenomena. She describes meetings with Yeats, Joyce, H.G. Wells and many others.

Isherwood, Christopher, *Ramakrishna and his Disciples*. New York: Touchstone/Simon & Schuster, 1965. The story of one of the principal mystics of the Hindu Renaissance in India.

Jung, C.G., *Memories, Dreams, Reflections*, Aniela Jaffe, ed. New York: Vintage, 1963. Jung concentrates on internal events, excluding most of the world changes and interpersonal occurrences that took place during his life. But, to someone with Jung's orientation, introspective awareness reveals more important material than recitation of historical facts. He includes dramatic visionary and paranormal experiences in his record.

Leary, Timothy, *High Priest*. New York: College Notes & Texts, 1968. His first autobiographical work, including encounters with William Burroughs, Richard Alpert (Baba Ram Dass), Allen Ginsberg and other psychedelic voyagers.

__________, *Jail Notes*. New York: Grove Press, 1970. The continuing saga, from inside jail this time, alternating between tough ''realism'' and visionary consciousness.

__________, *What Does WoMan Want?* Beverly Hills, CA: 88 Books, 1976. Leary merges autobiography with disguise and pure fiction in his portrayal of life as a sci-fi movie with himself as star. He includes more self-criticism than he has previously allowed into print, and gives his updated insights into the history and methodology of higher intelligence.

Kleps, Art, *Millbrook: The True Story of the Early Years of the Psychedelic Revolution*. See listing under ''Historical Intersections.''

Lilly, John C., *The Center of the Cyclone: An Autobiography of Inner Space*. New York: Bantam, 1973. His adventures with LSD, sensory isolation and the original Arica group.

Lilly, John C. and Antonietta Lilly, *The Dyadic Cyclone: The Autobiography of a Couple*. New York: Simon &

Schuster, 1976. Ranges from theoretical essays to recollections of severe illness, seen from the perspective of consciousness exploration. The first two chapters discuss their Arica training and the intrigues and politics which permeated it.

Peters, Fritz, *Boyhood with Gurdjieff*. Baltimore: Penguin, 1964. Early reminiscenses of day to day encounters with Gurdjieff, free from the ''school's'' jargon.

__________, *Gurdjieff Remembered*. New York: Samuel Weiser, 1965. Later meetings with Gurdjieff, again without the jargon and theory which make other tales about the teacher obscure.

Regardie, Israel, *The Eye in the Triangle: An Interpretation of Aleister Crowley*. St. Paul, MN: Llewellyn Publications, 1970. A look at Crowley as mystic, magician, poet and amateur psychologist by an author who regards the mage from a positive point of view. Regardie recognizes Crowley's numerous personal failings and the attention given them in other accounts. This book is an attempt to balance the record.

Roberts, Jane, *The Seth Material*. Englewood Cliffs, NJ: Prentice-Hall, 1970. A narrative of the author's unexpected initiation into all sorts of paranormal and altered state experiences, including, of course, meeting the ''entity'' who calls himself Seth.

Smith, Charlotte Fell, *John Dee*. London: Constable and Co., Ltd., 1909. The principal work to concentrate on the details of Dee's life. For another source on Dee, see Peter French's book in this section of the bibliography.

Stern, Paul J., *C.G. Jung: The Haunted Prophet*. New York: Delta, 1976. Stern reveals many details of Jung's life left out of the latter's memoirs. Stern takes a heavily critical stance toward Jung, but the portrait presented is not completely unsympathetic.

Strindberg, August, *From An Occult Diary*, ed. Torsten

Eklund, tr. Mary Sandbach. London: Icon Books Ltd., 1976. Madness appearing as altered states of consciousness and verging on the paranormal.

Swedenborg, Emanuel, *Heaven and Its Wonders and Hell*. New York: Swedenborg Foundation, 1974. The author's 18th century excursions into what he considered to be the after-death terrain.

__________, *The Journal of Dreams*, tr. James John Garth Wilkinson. *Studia Swedenborgiana*, Vol. 1, Nos. 1-4, 1974-1975. Swedenborg School of Religion, 48 Sargent St., Newton, MA 02158. A partial record of Swedenborg's dream and visionary experience.

Symonds, John, *The Great Beast: The Life and Magick of Aleister Crowley*. Mayflower Books Ltd., Frogmore, St. Albans, Herts AL2 2NF, England, 1973. A sardonic look at Crowley which brings out much of the mundane facts of his life. For a favorable treatment of Crowley, see Israel Regardie's book in this section of the bibliography.

Taft, Jessie, *Otto Rank*. New York: Julian Press, 1958. A thorough study of Rank's life and work, from his years as a young man through his membership in Freud's inner circle and on to his independent status as analyst and author.

Trobridge, George, *Swedenborg: Life and Teaching*. New York: Swedenborg Foundation, 1962. A sympathetic account of Swedenborg's life and teachings.

Watts, Alan, *In My Own Way: An Autobiography*. New York: Pantheon, 1972. Watts helped popularize Eastern philosophy. The philosophy shows up in this book along with accounts of meetings with the tremendous number of well-known people Watts encountered.

Williams, Gertrude Marvin, *Madame Blavatsky: Priestess of the Occult*. New York: Lancer Books, 1946. Interesting details of the life of one of the occult tradition's most colorful figures, presented from a critical point of view.

Disciplines of Self-Development

Anderson, Hilary, *Sri Aurobindo's Yoga of Transformation*. Publication not set. A comprehensive introduction to the major yogic disciplines of India, including Aurobindo's synthesis.

Bharati, Agehananda, *The Light At the Center: Context and Pretext of Modern Mysticism*. Santa Barbara, CA: Ross-Erikson, 1976. A radical approach to mysticism which fuses intimacy in all its forms, including sexual and psychedelic, with the total autonomy which mystical experience confers. The author is a scholar of religion and the social sciences, a Tantric (left-hand) initiate and a well-known professor of anthropology—one of the most unusual combinations around.

Bennett, J.G., *Gurdjieff: Making A New World*. New York: Harper & Row, 1973. A biography of Gurdjieff which focuses upon the ideas behind his life's work.

Crowley, Aleister, *De Arte Magica*. San Francisco: Level Press, n.d. A description of some of Crowley's sex magic techniques.

Evans-Wentz, W.Y., *Tibetan Yoga and Secret Doctrines*. New York: Oxford University Press, 1935. A compendium of several Tibetan yoga paths which have mystical experience as their goal.

King, Francis, *Sexuality, Magic and Perversion*. Secaucus, NJ: Citadel Press, 1971. The evolution of sexual forms of meditation, from Oriental to Western practice.

Leary, Timothy, *Neurologic*. n.p., 1973. Leary's model of the structure and developmental sequence of the evolved human nervous system.

Metzner, Ralph, *Maps of Consciousness*. New York: Collier Books, 1971. Interpretative and methodological comments regarding the I Ching, the Tarot, alchemy, astrology and Actualism.

Mishra, Rammurti S., *Yoga Sutras: The Textbook of Yoga Psychology*. Garden City, NJ: Anchor/Doubleday, 1963. A translation of Patanjali's classic aphorisms on yoga accompanied by Dr. Mishra's commentaries.

Sannella, Lee, *Kundalini: Psychosis or Transcendence?* H.S. Dakin Publications, 3101 Washington St., San Francisco, CA 94115, 1976. A physiological approach to the study of kundalini experiences by a researcher who believes in their transcendent character.

Dreams and Sleep

Donahoe, James J., *Dream Reality: The Conscious Creation of Dream & Paranormal Experience*. Oakland, CA: Bench Press, rev. ed., 1979. Transcending the waking/dream dichotomy by volitional exploration of special dream types, out-of-body experience, precognition and similar phenomena. Original experiences in these areas presented along with relevant methodologies.

Faraday, Ann, *Dream Power*. New York: Berkeley Medallion Books, 1973. A presentation of major dream interpretation strategies in action.

Garfield, Patricia, *Creative Dreaming*. New York: Simon & Schuster, 1974. An introduction to the use of lucid dreaming and ''Senoi'' techniques for therapeutic and aesthetic experience.

Green, Celia, *Lucid Dreams*. Institute of Psychophysical Research, 118 Banbury Road, Oxford, OX2 6JU, England, 1968. A comprehensive study of the subject which includes many original lucid dream accounts along with previously untranslated ones.

Hart, Hornell and Ella B. Hart, ''Visions and Apparitions Collectively and Reciprocally Perceived.'' *Proceedings of the Society for Psychical Research*, Vol. 41, pp. 205-249, 1932-1933. Case accounts from the files of the Society for Psychical Research concerning apparitions and mutual dream content. Some of the apparitions mentioned involved people who were conscious of appearing to the percipient(s). The Harts discuss the phenomena and list the cases according to category (apparitions of the living, apparitions of the dead, etc.) and evidential quality.

McCreery, Charles, *Psychical Phenomena and the Physical World*. See listing under "Parapsychological Information."

McLeester, Dick, *Welcome to the Magic Theater: A Handbook for Exploring Dreams*. Food for Thought Publications, P.O. Box 331, Amherst, MA 01002, 1976. An annotated bibliography of books which concern dreaming, along with McLeester's own insights and commentaries.

Moody, Jon, "The Martial Art of Dreaming." *Singularities* Special Report, 1978. A service of *Singularities: Advances in Psychology, Parapsychology, Medicine and Related Disciplines*. Bench Press, P.O. Box 24635, Oakland, CA 94623. An account of some unusual experiments in which the experimenters joined consciously-directed dreaming with techniques from the martial arts, thus eliciting both altered state and paranormal experiences.

Reed, Henry, "Meditation and Lucid Dreaming: A Statistical Relationship." *Sundance Community Dream Journal*, Vol. 2, No. 2, 1978. Data indicating the possible usefulness of meditation for increasing the incidence of lucid dreams. See entry below.

Reed, Henry and Dick Kohr, "Identifying Factors Influencing Dream Recall." *Sundance Community Dream Journal*, Vol. 2, No. 2, 1978. A checklist of recall-enhancing factors for dreamers who want to identify and encourage such factors. The *Sundance Community Dream Journal* (P.O. Box 595, Virginia Beach, VA 23451) regularly features articles on artistic, psychodynamic, and paranormal approaches to dreaming, along with writings which integrate dream studies with the Edgar Cayce material.

Schacter, Daniel L., "The Hypnagogic State: A Critical Review of the Literature." *Psychological Bulletin*, Vol. 83, No. 3, pp. 452-481, 1976. A review of the laboratory studies of the hypnagogic (pre-sleep) state.

Sparrow, Gregory Scott, *Lucid Dreaming: Dawning of the Clear Light*. Virginia Beach, VA: A.R.E. Press, 1974. The evocation of lucid dreaming as a means to further meditative experience during sleep.

Ullman, Montague and Stanley Krippner with Alan Vaughan, *Dream Telepathy*. New York: Macmillan, 1973. The experiments in dream telepathy and precognition conducted at the Maimonides Dream Laboratory in Brooklyn, New York.

Van Dusen, Wilson, *The Presence of Other Worlds: The Findings of Emanuel Swedenborg*. New York: Harper & Row, 1974. Van Dusen explores the processes of the hypnagogic state in addition to other realms inspired by Swedenborg's journals.

Fiction

Ayrton, Michael, *Fabrications*. New York: Holt, Rinehart & Winston, 1972. Irony and paradox concerning history, mythology, the arts and personal identity.

Brunner, John, *The Shockwave Rider*. New York: Ballantine, 1975. The hero, a fugitive from a state-subsidized school for geniuses, uses cybernetic wizardry in an attempt to further international democracy.

__________, *Stand on Zanzibar*. New York: Ballantine, 1968. Future perspectives on education, religion, urban insanity, the paranormal and international politics.

Burroughs, William S., *Nova Express*. New York: Grove Press, 1964. Word and image control exposed as the keys to a planetary ignition.

Crowley, Aleister, *Diary of a Drug Fiend*. New York: Samuel Weiser, 1973. Heights and depths of opiate and cocaine excess, with the attendant problems ''solved'' by the judicious use of magic.

Dick, Philip K., *The Three Stigmata of Palmer Eldritch*. Middlesex, England: Penguin Books, 1964. A drug appears which allows any ingester to literally change his or her own past. A meditation on the potential implications of godhood.

Fowles, John, *The Magus*. Boston: Little, Brown, 1965. The magus trip delineated: one version of the godgame.

Frayn, Michael, *Sweet Dreams*. New York: Ballantine, 1973. An ironic tale of a man who enters (take your pick): a dream, the after-death state or some other singularity.

__________, *A Very Private Life*. New York: Dell, 1968. A young lady of the future, dissatisfied with her family cubicle, her holovision, and the available psychotropic drugs (taken by parents and children alike, on nearly every occasion), runs away to experience the "Outside."

Gaddis, William, *JR*. New York: Alfred A. Knopf, 1975. JR, a sixth-grader, takes his conquering strides through the world of multinational business. A large cast of contrasting personalities becomes drawn into JR's orbit. Among the characters is a genius or two who can recognize the unholy intersection of economics with history and art.

Hesse, Hermann, *Steppenwolf*. New York: Bantam, 1963. A middle-aged German intellectual finds the way to higher consciousness through adventures much more accessible now, 50 years after this prophetic book's first publication.

Joyce, James, *Ulysses*. New York: Vintage Books, 1938. A day in the life of Dublin and the world; the wanderings of a father and son through myth made history.

__________, *Finnegans Wake*. New York: Viking, 1939. A cross-fertilization of world languages and tales. Joyce reels around the world/dream.

Lem, Stanislaw, *The Star Diaries*. Michael Kandel, tr. New York: Avon, 1976. The galactic travels of a parodic figure. (Of all the Voyages recounted by the narrator, the 20th and 21st are the most relevant to my discussion.)

Lessing, Doris, *Briefing for a Descent into Hell*. New York: Bantam, 1971. A professor stumbles into visionary understanding and experience under the guise of madness.

__________, *The Four-Gated City*. New York: Bantam, 1969. Martha Quest in the transition from England's cold war climate of the 1950's to the apocalyptic future.

Murphy, Michael, *Jacob Atabet: A Speculative Fiction*. Millbrae, CA: Celestial Arts, 1977. A man sets out on the adventure of psychophysical transformation, with the help of a few friends and with an extensive knowledge of the spiritual traditions which emphasize the embodiment of godhood.

Pynchon, Thomas, *The Crying of Lot 49*. New York: Bantam, 1966. The book's heroine encounters plots (some political, all of them literary) and heterodox communications networks in her search for a definitive revelation.

__________, *Gravity's Rainbow*. New York: Bantam, 1973. An encyclopedic work which connects and disbands physics, information theory, Pavlovian psychology, psychopharmacology, Wagner's Ring cycle, organic chemistry and multinational economics in the theater of World War II. Some characters guide plots of tremendous magnitude which involve those disenfranchised people willing to retaliate with counter-plots of their own. This conflict advances the story while threatening (successfully?) to unmake it.

Roberts, Jane, *The Education of Oversoul Seven*. Englewoods Cliffs, NJ: Prentice-Hall, 1973. The adventures of four characters who, while living in different times, find their lives intersecting through dreams, out-of-body experiences and Oversoul Seven.

Stapledon, Olaf, *Odd John*. New York: Dover, 1936. A mutant child with extraordinary psychic and intellectual powers locates others like himself. Under the boy's leadership, the group's members define themselves as a new species and decide to supplant Homo Sapiens.

Vonnegut, Kurt, *Slapstick*. New York: Delacorte, 1976. Dr. Wilbur Daffodil-11 Swain, an ex-President of the United States, reminisces about his childhood adventures with his twin genius sister, and the events which brought him to the Presidency and the country to tribalistic disintegration.

Wilson, Colin, *The Mind Parasites*. Oakland, CA: Oneiric Press, 1967. Some pioneers in consciousness research encounter and overcome the ''mind parasites'' that seem to resist human evolutionary progress.

__________, *The Philosopher's Stone*. New York: Warner, 1969. Also a story about a group of experimenters who attempt to further human evolution through consciousness research. They find a useful distinction between ecstasy and the heightened capacity for conscious intent. Some H.P. Lovecraft turns of plot appear here, as in *The Mind Parasites*.

Wyndham, John, *The Midwich Cuckoos*. New York: Ballantine, 1957. Children born with golden eyes show strong paranormal abilities, and learn with the help of a telepathic, shared consciousness. They struggle against the rest of the world, with the results typical of this genre.

Historical Intersections

Ariès, Philippe, *Western Attitudes Toward Death: From the Middle Ages to the Present*. Baltimore: John Hopkins University Press, 1974. Aries traces the transition in attitudes towards the death of oneself and those one loves by examining the evidence of funeral monuments, historical changes in the rituals surrounding death, and the treatment of death in literary works.

Blofeld, John, *The Secret and Sublime: Taoist Mysteries and Magic*. New York: E.P. Dutton, 1973. A review of Taoist practices including those directed towards self-transformation, the attainment of longevity, and the prize of immortality, as well as a brief survey of Taoist mystical philosophy.

Ellenberger, Henri F., *The Discovery of the Unconscious: The History and Evolution of Dynamic Psychiatry*. New York: Basic Books, 1970. Psychological theory and practice from early shamanism through Freud, Adler and Jung. Ellenberger makes a good case for the view that psychoanalysis and its descendants mark a return to the diversity of therapeutic forms characterized by the ancient mystery schools.

Harner, Michael J., ed., *Hallucinogens and Shamanism*. New York: Oxford University Press, 1973. Essays on the use of psychedelic substances in the Americas (primarily as part of shamanistic traditions in various tribal cultures), and in European witchcraft, written by anthropological researchers.

Koestler, Arthur, *The Case of the Midwife Toad*. New York: Vintage, 1973. The life and work of Austrian biologist Paul Kammerer, who attempted, perhaps successfully, to demonstrate the inheritance of acquired characteristics. Kammerer also maintained a long-time interest in meaningful coincidences. His ''law of seriality'' was the predecessor of C.G. Jung's theory of ''synchronicity.''

Kleps, Art, *Millbrook: The True Story of the Early Years of the Psychedelic Revolution*. Oakland, CA: Bench Press, 1977. The historical, comedic and philosophical aspects of the psychedelic voyage. Kleps describes his adventures with Timothy Leary, Richard Alpert (Baba Ram Dass) and company as they struggle for power, glory and enlightenment on the Hitchcock estate (Millbrook) and elsewhere.

Mishlove, Jeffrey, *The Roots of Consciousness: Psychic Liberation through History, Science and Experience*. New York: Random House, 1975. A survey of consciousness research and parapsychological studies, from early religious traditions to contemporary experimentation.

Podmore, Frank, *From Mesmer to Christian Science; A Short History of Mental Healing*. New Hyde Park, NY: University Books, 1963. Mesmer's theories and the movements which sprang from them.

Wasson, R. Gordon, *Soma: Divine Mushroom of Immortality*. New York: Harcourt Brace Jovanovich, 1972. A comprehensive argument to the effect that the amanita muscaria mushroom was not only the *soma* of the Vedas, but also the inspiration for religions and rites of Iran, China and Siberia.

Wasson, R. Gordon, Albert Hofmann and Carl A.P. Ruck, *The Road to Eleusis: Unveiling the Secret of the Mysteries*. New York: Harcourt Brace Jovanovich, 1978. Evidence for the idea that the Eleusinian Mysteries, practiced for nearly 2,000 years, depended upon the ingestion of psychedelic substances.

Wilson, Colin, *The Occult: A History*. New York: Random House, 1973. Short biographies of the major figures of the occult tradition such as John Dee, Mesmer, Rasputin, Crowley, Blavatsky, Gurdjieff and others. Wilson makes the case that the intensification of conscious volition forms the key to higher evolutionary potentials, including paranormal abilities.

Yates, Frances A., *Giordano Bruno and the Hermetic Tradition*. New York: Vintage, 1964. The importance of the magical tradition in Renaissance history and thought, and the relationship of that tradition to the eventual reign of science.

__________, *The Rosicrucian Enlightenment*. Boston: Routledge & Kegan Paul, 1972. The major influences surrounding and produced by the imaginary Rosicrucian secret society. In this and other books, Yates points out the role of Renaissance thought in the structure of contemporary occult systems and in the birth of the scientific world view.

Out-of-the-Body Experiences

Fox, Oliver, *Astral Projection: A Record of Out-of-the-Body Experiences*. Secaucus, NJ: Citadel Press, 1962. The author's accounts of his consciously induced out-of-the-body experiences. Fox does not attempt to verify his OOB's by checking them out for parapsychological content, but he does give precise descriptions of his experiments.

Green, Celia, *Out-of-the-Body Experiences*. New York: Ballantine, 1968. A detailed study of contemporary OOB's based upon the reports on file with the Institute of Psychophysical Research in Oxford, England.

Greenhouse, Herbert B., *The Astral Journey*. Garden City, NY: Doubleday, 1975. A historical review of reported OOB's, including many anecdotal accounts, which extends up to contemporary laboratory research.

Monroe, Robert A., *Journeys Out of the Body*. New York: Anchor, 1971. Monroe's own experiments, both involuntary and induced varieties.

Muldoon, Sylvan J. and Hereward Carrington, *The Projection of the Astral Body*. New York: Samuel Weiser, 1974. This book, first published in 1929, contains the then young Muldoon's many experiments with OOB's and his theories about the phenomenon.

Paradigms in Transition

Green, Celia, *The Decline and Fall of Science*. Institute of Psychophysical Research, 118 Banbury Road, Oxford, OX2 6JU, England, 1976. Green takes on psychology, lucid dreams, physics, medicine, parapsychology and a half-dozen other subjects to show the way around the large obstacles which inhibit frontier research.

Hardy, Alister, Robert Harvie and Arthur Koestler, *The Challenge of Chance: A Mass Experiment in Telepathy and Its Unexpected Outcome*. New York: Vintage, 1975. A call for the reevaluation of the concept of randomness supported by experimental details and a discussion of ''meaningful coincidences.''

Hume, David, *A Treatise of Human Nature*, ed. L.A. Selby-Bigge. London: Oxford University Press, 1897. A famous philosopher confronts the ultimate uncertainty of human knowledge and demonstrates that the existence of cause and effect relationships is something that people assume rather than prove.

Jung, C.G., *Synchronicity: An Acausal Connecting Principle*, tr. R.F.C. Hull. Princeton, NJ: Princeton University Press, 1973. Jung's identification of the important principle underlying "meaningful coincidences," and his comments on the relationship of this principle to the traditional ideas of causality and chance.

Koestler, Arthur, *The Roots of Coincidence: An Excursion into Parapsychology*. New York: Vintage, 1972. An investigation of the historical antecedents of Jung's theory of synchronicity and some recent formulations of the concept. Koestler draws material from mathematics and physics to show the inadequacies of classical probability theory and he suggests that studies of "synchronicity" may point the way out.

Kuhn, Thomas S., *The Structure of Scientific Revolutions*. Chicago: University of Chicago Press, 1970. A discussion of how fundamental changes in the prevailing scientific world-view come about.

Pearce, Joseph Chilton, *The Crack in the Cosmic Egg: Challenging Constructs of Mind and Reality*. New York: Pocket Books, 1971. Cultural "imperatives" regarding what is possible for human beings, and ways around such strictures.

Thompson, William Irwin, *Darkness and Scattered Light*. Garden City, NY: Anchor, 1978. Thompson's visions of the planetary future, arising from his understanding of history and his appreciation for myth.

Parapsychological Information

Bayless, Raymond, *Apparitions and Survival of Death*. Secaucus, NJ: University Books, 1973. The author cites various well-documented cases of apparitions to support the "survival hypothesis."

Donahoe, James J., *Dream Reality: The Conscious Creation of Dream and Paranormal Experience*. See description in the "Dreams and Sleep" section of this bibliography.

Flournoy, Theodore, *From India to the Planet Mars: A Study of a Case of Somnambulism with Glossolalia*. See under "Psychological Perspectives."

Gooch, Stan, *The Paranormal*. New York: Harper & Row, 1978. Gooch, author of *Total Man*, proposes that paranormal events be viewed as manifestations of "trance-work," imagination in action. He emphasizes the importance of personal experimentation in the study of the paranormal and considers some of the physiological and evolutionary aspects of the field.

Hart, Hornell and Ella B. Hart, "Visions and Apparitions Collectively and Reciprocally Perceived." See entry under "Dreams and Sleep" section of the bibliography.

Heywood, Rosalind, *Beyond the Reach of Sense: An Inquiry into Extra-sensory Perception*. New York: E.P. Dutton, 1974. An overview of the history of psychical research. The chapters on "cross-correspondences" describe a series of experiments designed to prove survival of death. This series was seemingly devised by the three founders of the SPR (Society for Psychical Research) after their deaths!

McCreery, Charles, *Psychical Phenomena and the Physical World*. New York: Ballantine, 1973. McCreery relates many interesting, original accounts of lucid dreams which he brings together with reports of OOB's, apparitions and psychokinesis. He shows how such phenomena do not present any greater violation of logical thought than do comparatively "ordinary" events.

__________, *Science, Philosophy and ESP*. Institute of Psychophysical Research, 118 Banbury Road, Oxford, OX2 6JU, England, 1967. The first part of the book concerns some particularly unusual reports from the annals of psychical research. In Part II, McCreery puts forward a theory of ESP which details how ESP might be demonstrated under conditions "repeatable" enough to satisfy the differing definitions of that word.

Myers, F.W.H., *Human Personality and Its Survival of Bodily Death*, ed. Susy Smith. Secaucus, NJ: University Books, 1961. This is a condensation of the original two-volume work published in 1903. Myers, a founder of the Society for Psychical Research, sums up his life's work in this writing, a classic of both psychology and parapsychology. Numerous cases of unusual psychological and paranormal phenomena are cited in the book, and Myers discusses their implications for an understanding of human personality that incorporates the higher aspects of human possibility as well as the normal and subnormal ones.

Osis, Karlis, and Erlendur Haraldsson, *At the Hour of Death*. New York: Avon, 1977. An extensive study of the experiences of the dying, including those who return from the verge of death to describe their vision of the after-life.

Owen, Iris M., and Margaret Sparrow, *Conjuring up Philip: An Adventure in Psychokinesis*. New York: Pocket Books, 1976. The story of a group's reportedly successful attempts to produce paranormal raps and table movements by creating a fictitious "ghost."

Roberts, Jane, *Adventures in Consciousness: An Introduction to Aspect Psychology*. Englewood Cliffs, NJ: Prentice-Hall, 1975. The continuing explorations of the author of *The Seth Material* (see "Autobiography and Biography") and her ideas about the nature of inner guides, reincarnational memory and other examples of what she calls "unofficial events."

Rogo, D. Scott, *The Welcoming Silence: A Study of Psychical Phenomena and Survival of Death*. Secaucus, NJ: University Books, 1973. Rogo's arguments for the survival of death include evidence from out-of-the-body experiences, death-bed visions, mediumship and other lines of psychical research.

Stevenson, Ian, *Twenty Cases Suggestive of Reincarnation*. Charlottesville, VA: University Press of Virginia,

1974. A cross-section of Stevenson's massive investigation into verifiable reincarnational memories.

Taylor, John, *Superminds*. New York: Warner, 1975. Accounts of the author's experiments regarding psychokinesis.

Tyrrell, G.N.M., *Apparitions*. New York: Collier, 1953. The author presents his theory on the origin of apparitions as well as his ideas on a number of related parapsychological subjects.

Ullman, Montague and Stanley Krippner with Alan Vaughan, *Dream Telepathy*. See under "Dreams and Sleep."

Psychological Perspectives

Ashley, Richard, *Cocaine: Its History, Uses and Effects*. New York: Warner, 1975. A study of the psychological, pharmacological and historical aspects of cocaine use.

Barber, T.X., "Suggested ('hypnotic') Behavior: The Trance Paradigm Versus an Alternative Paradigm." Medfield Foundation Report #103. Harding, MA: Medfield Foundation, 1970. A comprehensive, 66-page paper by one of the principal proponents of the nonstate view of "hypnosis." Barber details why he believes that the "hypnotic state" is a misnomer for intensified, waking responsiveness.

Barber, Theodore X. and Wilfried De Moor, "A Theory of Hypnotic Induction Procedures." *The American Journal of Clinical Hypnosis*, Vol. 15, No. 2, pp. 112-135, 1972. A concise discussion of "hypnotic" induction from the nonstate viewpoint.

Barber, T.X., N.P. Spanos and J.F. Chaves, *'Hypnosis', Imagination, and Human Potentialities*. Elmsford, NY: Pergamon, 1974. A comparison of the traditional and nonstate views of "hypnosis" which includes comments on how the new paradigm can be applied to the development of human possibilities.

Flournoy, Theodore, *From India to the Planet Mars: A*

Study of a Case of Somnambulism with Glossolalia. New Hyde Park, NY: University Books, 1963. A classic psychological investigation of a case of mediumship, conducted by the author, who was both a friend of William James and a believer in the paranormal. The phenomena produced by the medium whom Flournoy investigated show supernormal memory and subconscious playfulness rather than veridical, parapsychological perceptions.

Gooch, Stan, *Total Man*. New York: Ballantine, 1972. The role of polarities (including those in religion, language and the nervous system) in the evolution of the human psyche and brain.

__________, *The Neanderthal Question*. Wildwood House Ltd., 1 Prince of Wales Passage, 117 Hampstead Road, London NW1 3EE, England, 1977. The author explores in detail a theme from his earlier work, *Total Man*: the importance of the Neanderthal's characteristics and fate for studies of the past and future evolution of human personality.

Hunt, Harry T. and Cara M. Chefurka, "A Test of the Psychedelic Model of Altered States of Consciousness." *Archives of General Psychiatry*, Vol. 33, pp. 867-876, 1976. Details of an experiment in which subjects elicited strong changes in their perceptual awareness merely by attending to their environment in a receptive fashion.

Keen, Sam, *Voices and Visions*. New York: Perennial, 1974. The Psychology Today interviews with nine explorers of consciousness and culture, among them Norman O. Brown and Joseph Campbell.

Lindner, Robert, *The 50-Minute Hour*. New York: Bantam, 1954. The most relevant chapter here is the last one, "The Jet-Propelled Couch," which describes psychoanalyst Lindner's seduction by a patient's fantasy world.

Luria, A.R., *The Mind of a Mnemonist*. New York: Avon, 1968. A Russian psychologist's description of one of his patients, a man who was literally unable to forget anything.

Pearce, Joseph Chilton, *Magical Child: Rediscovering Nature's Plan for Our Children*. New York: E.P. Dutton, 1977. The vast creative resources available to children and adults, including paranormal abilities, and how they can be let free.

Smith, Adam, *Powers of Mind*. New York: Ballantine, 1976. Smith's personal encounters with researchers and research from both sides of the contemporary paradigm.

Spanos, Nicholas P. and Theodore X. Barber, "Behavior Modification and Hypnosis." A chapter from *Progress in Behavior Modification*, Vol. 3, ed. M. Hersen et al., pp. 1-44. New York: Academic Press, 1976. A critique of the "hypnotic state" construct and a comparison of "hypnotism" and behavior modification in action.

Szasz, Thomas, *Heresies*. Garden City, NY: Anchor, 1976. Aphorisms on the politics of metaphor and, consequently, the politics of psychotherapy.

————, *The Second Sin*. Garden City, NY: Anchor, 1974. The social implications of the use and abuse of language.

Tart, Charles T., ed., *Altered States of Consciousness*. New York: Anchor, 1972. The most relevant parts of the book are the sections entitled "Dream Consciousness" and "Hypnosis," and the chapter on the Erickson-Huxley "hypnosis" experiments.

Wilson, Colin, *New Pathways in Psychology: Maslow and the Post-Freudian Revolution*. New York: Taplinger, 1972. The rediscovery of the importance of human volition in contemporary psychology and philosophy and this discovery's implications for the higher possibilities of human nature.

Wilson, Sheryl C. and Theodore X. Barber, "The Creative Imagination Scale as a Measure of Hypnotic Responsiveness: Applications to Experimental and Clinical Hypnosis." *The American Journal of Clinical Hypnosis*, Vol. 20, No. 4, pp. 235-249, April 1978. A scale for measuring "suggestibility" based upon a non-authoritarian and positive model of "creative imagination," the authors' phrase for "hypnosis."

Visions and Commentaries

Brown, Norman O., *Closing Time*. New York: Random House, 1973. Brown interweaves Vico's history with *Finnegans Wake* to delineate a new science for any time.

__________, *Love's Body*. New York: Vintage, 1966. With a large company of fellow authors to draw from, Brown intersects and originates epigraphs moving from psychoanalysis to metahistory.

De Mille, Richard, *Castaneda's Journey: The Power and the Allegory*. Santa Barbara, CA: Capra Press, 1976. An evaluation of the factual and fictional bases of Castaneda's books.

Graves, Robert, *The White Goddess: A Historical Grammar of Poetic Myth*. New York: Farrar, Straus and Giroux, 1972. Graves searches out traces of the Great Goddess through Welsh, Celtic, Greek and other mythologies to proclaim her glories as Muse of the poet.

Guillaumont, A., et. al., trs., *The Gospel According to Thomas*. New York: Harper & Row, 1959. This book contains the original Coptic along with the English translation of one volume of the Nag-Hammadi Library, discovered in Egypt around 1945. According to the translators, this form of the Gospel is a translation or adaptation of a manuscript circa 140 A.D. This raises the possibility that this Gospel equals or excels the historical accuracy of all the four traditional Gospels. Many of the sayings herein mirror the understanding presented in Nagarjuna's Buddhism. They show a clearly different understanding of Christ's teachings regarding resurrection, religious tradition, the Second Coming and other matters than the most liberal reading of Christian orthodox teaching would provide.

Jodorowsky, Alexandro, *El Topo: A Book of the Film*. New York: Douglas Book Corporation, 1971. A scene by scene narrative of the film with many pictures taken from it, and an interview with Jodorowsky, the writer, director and principal actor, about myth and spiritual illumination.

Kleps, Art, *The Boo-Hoo Bible*. Neo-American Church, Box 600, Redway, CA 95560, 1971. Essays on synchronicity, illuminating cartoons and Neo-American Church memorabilia, all meant to communicate an iconoclastic and psychedelic sensibility.

Slade, Joseph W., *Thomas Pynchon*. New York: Warner, 1974. An appreciative contemplation of Pynchon's written works.

Wilhelm, Richard, tr., *The I Ching (Book of Changes)*, translated into English by Cary F. Baynes. Princeton, NJ: Princeton University Press, 1969. The classic Chinese manual for deciphering synchronicity. Carl Jung's foreword remains timely.

Index

SINGULARITIES

Advances in psychology, parapsychology,
medicine and the humanities.

Editor: James J. Donahoe, Ph.D.

SINGULARITIES is a newsletter which presents advances in a variety of areas. It offers previously unpublished research, reports from pioneers in the field, significant lab and field findings, commentaries on major discoveries and reviews of important books. SINGU-LARITIES articles include:

Autism & Acupressure
Mutual Dreams: A Breakthrough in Dreaming
Marijuana as Medicine
Hypnosis: New Paradigm, Major Breakthroughs
Secret TM Levitation Formula Revealed?
The Problem of Pain: Advances in Chemistry
Senoi Non-Dreamers
Astrology Investigation Yields Positive Correlations
Martial Artists Use Dream Techniques
Paranormal Healing of Cancer in Mice Reported
Biological Avenues to the City of Immortality

Regular columns include: Book Reviews, Aphorisms, Med/Pharm Reports, and Newsnotes.

SINGULARITIES also publishes Special Reports which go into greater detail on topics related to those covered in the newsletter.

Subscription Information:

SINGULARITIES is published at least 6 times a year. Make check or money order payable to Bench Press, $10 for 10 issues in North America. All other continents, $16. Check or money order should be made payable in U.S. Currency.

Send a stamped, self-addressed envelope if you would like a sample issue and a current listing of Special Reports.

Write to: SINGULARITIES, Bench Press, P.O. Box 24635, Oakland, CA 94623, U.S.A.

DREAM REALITY

The Conscious Creation of Dream
and Paranormal Experience

REVISED EDITION

by James J. Donahoe

Dr. Donahoe explores special dream states and psychic events which are revolutionizing our understanding of the nature of both dream and waking reality. Original experiences (including those of the author) in lucid dreaming, mutual dreams, out-of-body experience, precognition and other frontiers are presented along with methods the reader can use in personal experimentation.

"Donahoe is a serious, careful thinker and a bold explorer of inner space."

- Ann Faraday
New Age Journal

"One of the most remarkable books on the subject that I've ever read."

- Colin Wilson

"A good 'how to' journal. His advice to take responsibility for one's reality and thereby become a co-creator of the universe; to integrate the two polar modes of consciousness; and to reach beyond passivity, should bring gains to any reader who will try it. Non-sexist writing. Such a text is welcomed."

- Psychic

"A much needed bridge between the study of psychic phenomena and the insights of transpersonal psychology. Anyone at all interested in the field should give this book a thoughtful reading."

- Library Journal

Paperback - $3.95

To order direct, add $1.00 for shipping.
Available from: Bench Press
                  P.O. Box 24635
                  Oakland, CA 94623
                  U.S.A